"There is no more reliable voice today than Emily P. Freeman. Her consistency and faith have moved and changed me over and over again. *The Next Right Thing* is exactly that—the next right thing for you to read, for Emily to write, and for us all to live by. I'm so thankful this book exists."

Annie F. Downs, bestselling author of *100 Days To Brave*
and *Remember God*

"*The Next Right Thing* enlightened me, brought awareness, and gave me tools I didn't realize were missing in my decision-making. Emily points us to ultimate peace and clarity in our lives in the midst of uncertainty and chaos by gently pulling our focus back to the One who gives them."

Candace Cameron Bure, actress, producer,
and *New York Times* bestselling author

"This book will leave you with confidence, wisdom, intention, and a perspective shift about the big and small decisions in your life. Reading *The Next Right Thing* is your next right decision."

Myquillyn Smith, *Wall Street Journal* bestselling author
of *Cozy Minimalist Home*

"Emily has a gift for speaking into light things that are already true in most of us but are often dimmed by the clouds of busyness. Her words are a must-read in my own life, and I'm so grateful to call her a friend."

Tsh Oxenreider, author of *At Home in the World*

"Emily P. Freeman is the real deal. She is wise, a trusted guide, and prepared with just the words you need to hear at the moment you need to hear them. If you are feeling stuck or overwhelmed or are longing for a revitalizing perspective on decision-making that is both practical and life-changing, then *The Next Right Thing* is the book you have been searching for."

Mandy Arioto, president and CEO of MOPS International

"Like all of Emily's writing, this book is both insightful and practical. It teaches us that life is to be lived, not figured out. And the way we live it is one brave choice at a time."

Jeff Goins, bestselling author of *The Art of Work*

"Emily P. Freeman's voice is gentle yet mighty, and I'm obsessed with every word of this quiet masterpiece. We all find ourselves in times of transition, aching for a final decision, and it's easy to force the finish line. Emily kindly and confidently invites us to a new path where the finish line is secondary. I'll never make decisions the same way again."

Kendra Adachi, founder of The Lazy Genius Collective

"*The Next Right Thing* is a book you can go back to again and again, and each time it will hit you in a new and fresh way. If you struggle to make decisions, if you're in the midst of a big life change, if you'd just love some quiet guidance to be more intentional with your days, and/or if you love Emily's writing and podcast, this book is for you!"

Crystal Paine, *New York Times* bestselling author, founder of MoneySavingMom.com, and host of *The Crystal Paine Show*

"Reading Emily P. Freeman, I start to believe Jesus's promise more—that his yoke is easy and his burden light. *The Next Right Thing* delivers us from anxious hand-wringing over our uncertain futures."

Jen Pollock Michel, author of *Surprised by Paradox*

"Relatable, actionable, and inspiring, Emily's words will take you deeper into the process of graciously taking your next step."

Alan and Gem Fadling, founders of Unhurried Living

"Emily has become my decision-making guide. In this book she offers deep wisdom that is easily applied to everyday life. Emily shows us that the next right thing is not only possible but also desirable. This book is both timely and timeless."

James Bryan Smith, author of *The Good and Beautiful God*

"We live in a time with a crippling, overwhelming number of options and decisions to make. Emily offers a practical guide for discerning 'the next right thing' in the big and small moments of life. I am so grateful for this book!"

Jordan Raynor, bestselling author of *Called to Create*

*the*

# NEXT
# RIGHT
# THING

o o o

A SIMPLE, SOULFUL
PRACTICE FOR MAKING
LIFE DECISIONS

## EMILY P. FREEMAN

Revell

*a division of Baker Publishing Group*
Grand Rapids, Michigan

Published by Revell
a division of Baker Publishing Group
PO Box 6287, Grand Rapids, MI 49516-6287
www.revellbooks.com

Printed in the United States of America

Library of Congress Cataloging-in-Publication Data
Names: Freeman, Emily P., 1977– author.
Title: The next right thing : a simple, soulful practice for making life decisions / Emily P. Freeman.
Description: Grand Rapids, MI : Revell, [2019]
Identifiers: LCCN 2018049161 | ISBN 9780800736521 (cloth)
Subjects: LCSH: Decision making—Religious aspects—Christianity. | Simplicity—Religious aspects—Christianity. | Self-actualization (Psychology)—Religious aspects—Christianity.
Classification: LCC BV4599.5.P75 F74 2019 | DDC 248.4—dc23
LC record available at https://lccn.loc.gov/2018049161

The author is represented by Alive Literary Agency, 7680 Goddard Street, Suite 200, Colorado Springs, CO 80920, www.aliveliterary.com.

19  20  21  22  23  24  25      7  6  5  4  3

For anyone who's ever made a pro/con list
in the middle of the night.

# CONTENTS

○ ○ ○

Contents

*one*

# DO THE NEXT
# RIGHT THING

o o o

*Most of us go through life praying a little,
planning a little, jockeying for position,
hoping but never being quite certain of
anything, and always secretly afraid that
we will miss the way.*

A. W. Tozer, *The Knowledge of the Holy*

The admissions building smells like initiative, angst, and Y2K. I stand at the entrance of my college alma mater just a few miles from my house and take a long, deep breath. *What am I even doing?* The question still lingers even though my decision is mostly made. The main desk sits in the center of the building, a large circular piece like a mouth wide open. Approaching the desk, I scan the room for familiar faces, glad when I see none. I'm not ready for a casual, small-talk conversation about why I'm here. The woman inside the eternal desk offers to help, and I tell her I would like a copy of my transcript. She gets to work, and I settle in a bit.

The one question people ask when they find out I am enrolling in grad school is why. It's a normal question, one I would ask you, too, if you told me the same thing. Why are you going back to school? This is the question that has kept me up at night for weeks while I made my decision. *Why would I want to do this? I have a job, a family, a full life already. This will take lots of time and lots of money, and what is the actual point?* It's the question that begged for an answer while I tried to decide what to do next. I didn't have a clear plan with bullet points, a job I wanted to get that required this degree, or even the cultural expectation you have when you decide to go to college the first time because "that's just what you do." At my age, going to school again is not just what you do. As I weighed this decision, I annoyed everyone around me. Or maybe I just annoyed myself. Sometimes it's hard for me to tell the difference.

It's the *mights* and *maybes* of our lives that keep us awake at night. *Maybe I should accept the new position. Which schooling choice is best for my kids? How can I support my aging parents? What might happen if I choose wrong?*

With my school decision, I just wasn't sure if it was right. My husband, John, was all for it, the timing was fine, I was interested in the course work. But what if I decided to do it and then it turned out to be too stressful for our family? Or what if I decided *not* to do it and regretted that decision too?

For months, the possibilities permeated every conversation I had with family and close friends. We all handle the pressure of decision-making differently, and this time I'd lost my way a bit, turning into a hyperfocused version of myself. Listening intently during sermons to see if God had a special message just for me in the words. Looking for deeper meanings in the pithy quotes on Dove chocolate candy wrappers. Googling *decision-making* every which way possible: *how to make a decision in five minutes, what to do when you have a big decision, how to know if you're choosing right.*

It doesn't matter what the specific decision is. Unmade decisions hold power. They pull, they push, they interrupt where they aren't wanted and poke us awake at night. They can turn us into strange versions of ourselves. Like toddlers at our feet right before dinner, they follow us around and refuse to leave us alone until we face them head-on and either pick them up or point them in the right direction. If only we knew what the right direction was.

Maybe that's where you find yourself now. You want to give this decision the attention it deserves, and you're willing to do the work. The only problem is, you don't know what work is required, and perhaps you don't think you have the time to learn.

○  ○  ○

When it comes to making decisions, chances are you've probably heard the advice this book is built upon before. The phrase isn't new or even particularly creative. Personally, it's advice I've taken, forgotten, and remembered again. But it's held me up through young motherhood, grief, indecision, frustration, vocational boredom, and spiritual confusion. A version of this advice has been famously quoted by Mother Teresa, Reverend Martin Luther King Jr., Theodore Roosevelt, and Anne Lamott. It's become a common catchphrase for coaches and athletes, in boardrooms and corporate motivational speeches. So, what is that advice? *Do the next right thing.*

The concept is perhaps most famously found in The Big Book of Alcoholics Anonymous: "We earnestly pray for the right ideal, for guidance in each questionable situation, for sanity, and for the strength to do the right thing."[1]

While we may not all be alcoholics, it's safe to say we all need guidance in each questionable situation, we all need the strength to do the right thing, and, in many ways, we are all addicted to something. There's nothing like an unmade decision to smoke our addictions out.

Maybe you are addicted to clarity and certitude, wanting to be absolutely sure of all the details before moving forward.

Maybe you value approval above all, wanting to seek everyone else's perspective before understanding your own, accounting for a lack of confidence and a chronic case of hesitation.

Maybe you have an aversion to making decisions so you either delegate them, avoid them, or make them too quickly just to get them settled.

Perhaps you're addicted to activity, to hustle, to the fast pace of a well-connected life, and so when a decision needs to be made that could change the course of your future, you don't have the space to consider what might be best, much less what you might actually want to do.

It's estimated that adults make over 35,000 decisions every day. A study at Cornell University revealed that Americans make over two hundred daily decisions on food alone.[2] So many of those decisions are mindless; we aren't actually aware of our choices. Right now chances are high that you have a decision to make. Those 35,000 decisions don't even account for the extra ones that come in the midst of a job loss, marriage proposal, graduation, diagnosis, cross-country move, promotion, argument, pregnancy, or car accident. Every day we have choices to make, priorities to set, goals to meet, and desires to consider.

Doing the next right thing is good advice, but it didn't sink in for me fully until I started noticing it in the Gospels. So often, right after Jesus performed a miracle, he gave a simple next thing to do.

To the leper, he said to tell no one, "But go and show yourself to the priest" (Luke 5:14).

To the paralytic, he said, "Get up, pick up your stretcher, and go home" (v. 24).

To Jairus and his wife, after raising their daughter from the dead, when he had their full and complete attention, and when chances were good he could get them to swear their lives away for his sake, he did not perform a lecture about dedicating their lives to him or about what grand plans he had for their girl now that she was alive. Instead, he told them to give her something to eat (8:55). After raising their daughter from the actual dead, the one thing Jesus told them in the face of their rapt attention was to go make lunch. At first glance, that seems like a waste of a captive audience.

Rather than a life plan, a clear vision, or a five-year list of goals, the leper, the paralytic, and Jairus and his wife were given clear instructions by Jesus about what to do next—and only *next*. Perhaps he knew something about our addiction to clarity. He knew if we could somehow wrangle a five-year plan out of him, we would take it and be on our merry way.

After Jesus performed miracles, he made the next right thing unmistakably clear. But what about for us? Let's take our cues from Jesus and the recovering alcoholics by considering what it means for us to do the next right thing *now*. Not the next big thing. Not the next impressive thing. Just the next right thing in front of us. So what is our next right thing? It's a question that gets my attention, and it's what I want to explore with you.

This is a book about making decisions. It's also a book about making a life. What a privilege it is to have a choice to make at all. We live in a world where many people don't have the luxury of choice in certain areas, and this book presupposes you are in a position in life where choices are yours to make. We all have a different degree of control over various areas of our lives, depending on our age, our season, our family life, and our degree of privilege because of our race, gender, financial situation—and so on forever. I'll invite you as you read to bring to mind those areas in your life where you do have a choice, no matter how small. Be willing to hold your choices with an open hand and see them from a different perspective.

Regardless of your own degree of personal choice, you have a God who walks and talks with you, who moves in and through you, who sings over you. How he moves in you may be different from how he moves in me, but one thing is certain. He remains unchanged. As my friend and teacher James Bryan Smith so kindly reminds us, you are one in whom Christ delights and dwells, and you live in the strong and unshakable kingdom of God. The decision is rarely the point. The point is you becoming more fully yourself in the presence of God.

○   ○   ○

Eventually I made my schooling decision and decided to enroll even though I couldn't articulate exactly why. I talked with my spiritual director about this when I was still in the deciding phase, and she said something I haven't forgotten. "Our Western minds are trained to go down the path of explaining. We think if we can understand it, then we can control it."

It's true, don't you think? We are conditioned to believe the only reason we should do things is if we know why, where we are headed, and for what purpose. No wonder we have trouble making decisions. If we don't have clear answers or sure things, then taking a big step feels like a risk at best and a wasteful mistake at worst.

*If I understand it, then I can control it.*

For me, in this particular decision, this is what I know: I feel a call to the deeper life with Jesus and with people, in my personal life and my ministry life and my business life. I'm not choosing a degree path because I feel like something is missing but because, finally, I can see the whole. And what my wholeheartedness has been telling me over the past few years is that I want to learn more about spiritual formation, I want to become more fully myself, and I want to do it alongside a community of people who want that too.

At the time of this writing, I still have a few months left until graduation. I'll be forty-two years old. During that period of time when I was trying to make the decision, my focus was on the decision itself, but I also noticed something shifting within me. I felt needy, open, aware, and ready to listen. At every turn, I was eager to hear from God. We know decisions are important because each one carries a consequence. Decisions shape our lives. But what we often overlook is not only how our choices shape outcomes but how they shape us too. They reveal our character and help to create our character.

What if the way we make decisions is equally as important as the decisions we make? What if choice is one of the primary avenues of our spiritual formation? Unmade decisions have the power to either close us up in fear or open us up to love. This is both the burden and the gift of our indecision. We get to choose which one we carry.

What these next chapters will do for you, I hope, if you take action, is create space within your soul and on your schedule for you to remember who you are, where you live, and why it matters. In turn, you'll learn to name the unnamed things within you and discern with God what your next right thing could be. Whether you are in the midst of a major life transition or if you simply suffer from the low-grade anxiety that daily life can sometimes bring, you always have decisions to make, big or small. As long as we live, we'll be making decisions. Like you, I want to make good ones. If you're facing something and you don't know where to start, maybe doing the next right thing will be a welcome beginning.

In the spirit of following this advice, each chapter will end with a short prayer followed by a simple practice. Some of these practices will invite you to answer a question and enter into a more contemplative posture. Others will be more tangible, like instructions to make a certain kind of list or take a particular action. These practices are meant to help you explore not only what your next right thing might be but also where God is with you in your indecision. If you find that certain practices aren't leading you closer to God, don't do them. The goal is not to finish an activity. The goal is always union with God.

## ○ A PRAYER

*O God, I am open.*
*The decisions I'm facing have become too much.*
*Ease my fatigue with your presence and my hesitation with your peace.*
*Here is an issue that has me tied up in knots. Will you begin to untangle me?*
*What do you want me to know today?*
*O God, I am open.*

## ○ A PRACTICE: PAY ATTENTION

What is something you're thinking about pursuing, starting, quitting, making, finishing, or embracing? If you don't see the clear path, the end game, or the five-year plan, take heart.

Be excessively gentle with yourself.

Get still.

Stop talking.

Pause the constant questioning of everyone else's opinion.

Now hold that thing, whatever it is, in your mind.

Pay attention to your body and your soul—*Does it rise or does it fall?*

# *two*

# BECOME A SOUL MINIMALIST

○　○　○

*Minimalism is not that you should own nothing. But that nothing should own you.*

Joshua Becker, *The More of Less*

A whispered chaos swirls in the mind of those who carry unmade decisions. I am never more open to advice, perspective, and other people's opinions than when I have a decision to make. I'm never more aware of my need for God, for hope, and for direction than when I have to make a choice. I'm open, I'm ready, I'm listening for any clue as to what I should do next.

When I have an important decision to make, my tendency is to get more input, not less. I approach my daily decisions and plans for the future like a hoarder gathering opinions, facts, perspectives, and lists. But what if I approached them like a minimalist: clearing space, quieting my mind, and listening for whispers in the silence? Would it make a difference?

When the answers aren't clear, what we want more than anything is peace, clarity, and a nudge in the right direction. The problem is we are often looking for direction in all the wrong places. Often the clues to our next decision remain within us, unheard and undiscovered. When we take the time to follow those clues, we might find out we are holding on to some things we no longer need and gripping some things we might need to let go.

Wouldn't it be freeing to take your next right step with a particular decision you are carrying—and to do it today? If that sounds good to you, I'd like to help you do that. And so we'll begin perhaps in an unlikely place, not by making a list but by clearing the decks.

If you're considering a decision and you're hoping this book will help, I want you to know that is my goal. I will not forget the reason you picked up this book. I will hold that in front of me as I write and remember this one thing well. I know the weight those unmade decisions carry, and I want to help you find some relief. In light of that, I will keep these chapters short and do my best to walk with you as you walk with God.

Often, before you can move forward, it's essential to practice doing the next small thing in front of you, like riding a bike before you drive a car. That's what becoming a soul minimalist is about. If there's one thing I know for sure in the kingdom of God it's this: the thing we often think is The Thing is often *not* the thing but is, in fact, only *a* thing. We come forward with a Huge Life Decision and we long for answers and direction. But we've got absolutely nothing, so we talk ourselves in circles and everything feels muddy and heavy and difficult. We pray and ask for advice and still, nothing rises to the surface as the right direction to go. What I'm finding to be most helpful more than any list, question, or sage advice is simply to get quiet in a room with Jesus on the regular, not for the sake of an answer but for the sake of love. I cannot promise your decision will be made with ease, but I can say that you'll remember love is the important thing. And when you have a big decision to make, you need all the love and support you can possibly get. The only place I know to find that for sure is in the presence of Jesus.

○　○　○

I recently watched a documentary on Netflix called *Minimalism: A Documentary About the Important Things*.[1] In it, a woman named Courtney Carver shared her story of being diagnosed with MS. She and her family traded fear among them at this difficult news, but instead of taking it easy, her instinct during that time was to work harder to prove she was okay. She overworked, overexercised, and basically overextended herself. As a result, she ended up feeling physically terrible. The advice she got from people who knew about MS was that she had to start listening to her body.

"Listen to my body?" she asked. "I can't even listen to my family; I don't know how I'm going to hear my body."

No matter how great that advice was, it wasn't helpful at first. She didn't know what it practically meant to listen to her body. But she went on to explain how her journey of simplifying her schedule and her home began to reduce the stress in her life. It provided her with the space she needed to begin to listen to her body and be more in tune with what really mattered. Her segment in that documentary stuck with me.

If we struggle to listen to our family, the people we see and love every single day, and the body we live in (and have since the day we were born), how much more, I wonder, do we all have trouble listening to what's happening on our soul level, that part of us we can't see at all, the part that only shows herself in the safest of circumstances? The world is run by worn-out people, and our soul is often lost beneath the piles of our everyday life. This idea of becoming a soul minimalist is not so different from being an actual minimalist.

As I was at the gym, listening to a podcast interview between authors Tsh Oxenreider and Joshua Becker, this idea of soul minimalism came to me for the first time. I've enjoyed Joshua's blog, *Becoming Minimalist*, for quite some time, and in this episode, he and Tsh had an easy conversation about simplicity and the difference between too much and enough. I immediately warmed to Joshua's perspective of *becoming* a minimalist, emphasizing how the journey is important even if we never quite arrive at the destination, something he was careful to acknowledge.[2]

At some point in their conversation, Joshua pointed out that we all have regular, seasonal input of stuff into our homes that comes by way of gifts, school papers, work projects, and various decorations depending on the celebration, but we don't often have regular output. As a result, the clutter builds up inside our houses. In a similar way, our soul receives frequent input with infrequent output. At the time I was listening to that interview, I was also walking on the treadmill in a crowded gym with not just one TV in front of me but eight all in a row. I could see the news, a game show, a basketball game, and a soap opera all at the same time.

Meanwhile, a woman in front of me pedaled fast on a stationary bike, two men to my left worked with those giant rubber band things I never know what to do with, and behind me I was aware of movement in the pool on the other side of the glass. Input was everywhere. In the midst of this highly stimulating exterior world, I made a discovery about my interior world: the input is automatic. So where is the output? How am I regularly getting rid of the soul clutter I no longer need?

The difficult conversation, the suspicious glance someone might give us, the thing we said we wish we could take back—these things are constantly happening every day, all day. Where is the output? How are we letting them go?

It isn't realistic to live in a constant state of simplicity. We are naturally complex creatures, made up of various systems: nervous, circulatory, digestive—not to mention the relationships, emotions, dreams, hurts, and desires that also shape us. All of these are part of our human existence and not one of them is simple. Complexity has its place. But when our souls are filled with clutter, what is meant to be complex and awe-inspiring can become complicated and exhausting. One of my favorite things Joshua Becker says about minimalism is that it's not enough to just declutter; we have to de-*own*.

While it's a powerful practice to apply that statement to your home, imagine what happens when you apply it to your soul. Becoming a soul minimalist does not mean that you should hold on to nothing but rather that nothing should have a hold on you.

When my soul feels like that crowded gym, with lots of movement, hurry, and input, it brings peace to embrace the concept of minimalism. I can't say what the result of this might be for you, but I can tell you for me, the best way to uncover a bit of white space in my own soul is to be still.

Stillness is to my soul as decluttering is to my home. Silence and stillness are how I sift through the day's input. The silence serves as a colander, helping me discern what I need to hold on to and allowing what I don't need to fall gently away, making space to access courage and creativity, quieting to hear the voice of God.

If you have trouble listening to your family, your body, or your soul, a good first step is to find small cracks of time to be silent and still. I know how hard this is. Author and pastor A. J. Swoboda points out that in the last ten years, we've gone from having a TV in our living rooms to having a TV in our pockets.[3] We know all the ways our phone seems intent on ruining our best efforts at silent stillness. I won't go too far down the road of all the ways our phones have rewired our brains, and I won't make arguments for the pros and cons of technology, but here's what I will say: if you are carrying an unmade decision, you have to find a way to push back the distraction of your phone and allow some nothing space to fill the in-between moments.

For me, that looked like turning off all notifications. Maybe you did this years ago, and if so, you're already ahead of the game. You already know it's a small step, but it's also a tiny declaration.

*Facebook, you do not get to interrupt me.*

*Instagram, you do not have my permission to tap me on the shoulder whenever you want to.*

*Headlines, I can read you all at once later. I do not need to know the moment news breaks.*

*Phone, you are not allowed to boss me. I have good work to do. I have a life to live. I have decisions to make.*

This mindset shift serves as a tangible invitation to your soul: *you are welcome to come out whenever you feel safe. And when you do, I'll pay attention.* Be relentless and unapologetic with your phone. Notifications are interrupting our day, our concentration, our focus, and our ability to be present. So let's just ignore them on purpose.

What's next? The specifics are up to you, but I would suggest a willingness to allow some space during the in-betweens of life where you don't allow yourself to check your phone. Maybe a walk where you leave it behind or a whole morning where you keep it turned off. Anything to help push back the darting eyes, the constant scrolling, and the brain space we willingly sacrifice on the tiny, shiny altar of our phone screens.

We're letting everyone else's agenda live for free in the sacred space of our creative mind, and it's time for an eviction. This space is necessary for ideas to form, for questions to rise up, for hope to weave her way into our vision for the future, and for the dots of decision to begin to connect in the quiet places of our mind and heart.

Good decisions require creativity, and creativity requires space. This space is necessary for you to speak out against the injustices you see in the world, the problems you know you can help solve, and the beauty you long to deliver. Of course our life is filled with natural interruptions and distractions, and this is often where our real life happens. But there is a whole category of distraction we have control over, and that's the stuff that comes from our phones. If you would like an even more concrete plan for a technology fast, author Andy Crouch, in his book *The Tech-Wise Family*, follows this rule: an hour a day, a day a week, and a week a year without technology.[4]

As you embrace your own version of becoming a soul minimalist, I hope you'll receive the wisdom to begin to give up what you no longer need, like fear about the future or regret over the past. I hope you'll embrace a willingness to face the silence within and not worry so much what you may or may not hear. I hope you'll be willing to create a little space for your soul to breathe so you can discern your next right thing in love.

o   o   o

As you continue to read about this simple, soulful practice of making decisions, there are two movements we'll keep coming back to over and over again throughout this book. The first is the concept we just talked about, that of becoming a soul minimalist—clearing clutter and creating space for silence, letting your soul know it's safe to come out, and making room to listen. The second movement I'll introduce in the next chapter, and that is the practice of holding space long enough to name the unnamed things. Let's begin to do that together.

## ○ A PRAYER

*We confess we live distracted lives, and our insides often shake with constant activity.*

*We have grown accustomed to ignoring our low-grade anxiety, thinking that it's just a normal part of an active life.*

*This might be typical, and it might be common. But let it not be normal.*

*Instead of trying to figure out how to calm the chaos and hustle around us, we rejoice with confidence that we don't have to figure our way back to the light and easy way of Jesus, because you have already made your way to us.*

*We have your Spirit living within us, which means there's hope for us after all.*

*You invite us into each moment to simply do the next right thing in love.*

## ○ A PRACTICE: **NOTICE THE SILENCE**

Silence may be more accessible than you think. Begin to notice the naturally silent spaces in your days—the first light of morning, your office space when you arrive early, the walk to the mailbox, your apartment before your roommate gets home from work, the drive to the grocery store. Rather than filling these times with sound, or holding on to the soul clutter by rehearsing past conversations or future possibilities, decide instead to let yourself be quiet inside the silence and see if your friend Jesus has anything to say.

# *three*
# NAME THE NARRATIVE

o  o  o

*We get into trouble whenever we do not name things properly.*

Ronald Rolheiser, *The Holy Longing*

draw the line at a female robot bossing me around.

Before the days of text messaging and voice mail, we had special machines whose sole job was to answer the phone in our absence. We called them answering machines, and that's exactly what they did. In college, my roommate and I had one that used actual full-size cassette tapes to record incoming messages, which meant if you called our dorm room, you could leave a four-hour-long message if you felt so inclined.

One day I came home and hit play to hear the messages. The first voice was that of a female robot telling me not to hang up because this could be the most important call of my life. Then "she" said her records indicated I may not have health insurance. She promised help was on the way if only I would press one now, but I should be prepared to experience a short wait due to the tremendous response. Basically she was telling me a robot wanted to change my life, but I was going to have to be patient.

Needless to say, I didn't press one. I wouldn't have pressed one even if I didn't have health insurance. Even if I needed the thing the robot was offering, I wouldn't have wanted it that way because I have no respect for a robot on my answering machine—which is essentially robots leaving messages for robots, if you really get down to it. When it comes to buying health insurance or doing any kind of business, we want to be able to talk to a person, someone who knows our name or, at the very least, someone who *has* a name.

Names are important. There's a reason we name babies when they're born. Beyond all the ancient and spiritual history behind naming, another reason is simply so we have a way to differentiate you from someone else. It's a way of identifying you, so when we call your name, you'll turn your head. When we refer to you, saying your name gives you a presence in the room even if you aren't there.

We named our first girl before we realized we were having twins. I had her name picked months before there were any babies at all. Her name is delicate and ladylike and lovely. But the day we found out I was carrying two girls, the pressure to pick a second name was heavy. I couldn't bear the thought of my girls within me, limbs pressing in on me and one another, one with a name and the other without. As we left the hospital, shiny black-and-white ultrasound photos clutched in my swollen hand, John and I chose a second name as we sat at a stoplight on Green Valley Road. We knew right away the name was a fit. Both our girls now had our love in the form of two beautiful names: Ava Grace and Anna Estelle.

It was powerful to name them before we met them. They may have come into this messy world with nothing, but at least here was proof they belonged. Jesus calmed Martha by saying her name twice. He changed Simon's name to Peter, the rock. He added the "ha" to Abram, literally putting *Yahweh, the sound of God* into Abraham's name. And after his resurrection, Mary mistook Jesus for the gardener until he spoke her name. His attention is turned not toward politics, policy, or programming but toward people and their names.

Names mean things; they carry weight and importance and intimacy. To know a person's name is to know something of them. The world is not a nameless, faceless green-and-blue mass of land and water. The world is made of people, rich with story, full of intrigue, longing for passion and love and adventure. Knowing people begins with knowing their name. In her book *Walking on Water*, Madeleine L'Engle says "our names are part of our wholeness. To be given a name is an act of intimacy as powerful as any act of love."[1]

If naming can do all that—christen us into life and release new growth—is the opposite also true? Could allowing things to remain unnamed and unacknowledged hold the life back? Naming is powerful when it comes to people. But it's powerful for other things as well.

Maybe a reason why a particular decision you are carrying today feels difficult is because there are things beneath the surface that remain unnamed within you, things you either haven't acknowledged or would rather ignore. Sometimes indecision is the result of a busy schedule or a hesitant personality. Other times it's because something within us remains unnamed, and we simply don't have enough information or self-knowledge to move forward.

Without a name, we can't be specific. And there's nothing fear likes more than non-specificity. We have an enemy who loves to cloud our minds over with generalities and a vague sense of anxiety. No wonder we can't make a decision. Let's begin to create space for the naming and, in turn, a more gently informed decision-making process.

○　○　○

On July 26, 2014, medical missionary Nancy Writebol became one of the first Americans diagnosed with the Ebola virus in West Africa. I followed her story in the news, and months later, once she had recovered, I paid attention when I noticed she and her husband were preparing to make a statement to the press.

I had read about how at first she didn't know it was the Ebola virus; she thought it was "just malaria." (I suppose when you have to choose between Ebola and malaria, it makes sense to put a *just* in front of *malaria*.) But once they learned it was Ebola, she had to be quarantined in the house where she was living. She was grateful for the window in her room so her husband could stand on the other side and talk to her through it.

When the Writebols appeared on TV for a news conference, Nancy's husband spoke first, sharing his gratitude for all the prayers and support. With a pleasant look on his face, he continued to tell the story of how he read from Philippians to his wife while she was sick and how they deeply identified with Paul in that particular book. This may not have been the assignment they had planned, but they took it as an assignment nevertheless.

When it was Nancy's turn to speak, she shared similar words of thanksgiving, love, and gratitude. She spoke with compassion about her friends back in West Africa, and she asked viewers to continue to pray for them.

I don't know the Writebols personally, but I adored them immediately. They seemed like lovely and gracious people. Soon the screen split between the Writebols and the CNN commentators, and I watched to get their reaction to the couple.

CNN medical correspondent Elizabeth Cohen began to speak. "It's interesting that it would be very easy for their narrative to be one of traumatization. She has been through a lot. She said many times, 'I thought *I'm not going to make it anymore.*' But it's not a narrative of trauma. It's a narrative of joy. We can all learn from that."[2]

*It's not a narrative of trauma. It's a narrative of joy.*

When the news conference was over, I couldn't get that phrase out of my head. And now, years later, it still lingers. If you are struggling to discern your next right thing, maybe it's because you feel stuck in an unnamed time of transition, of waiting, of grief, or even of some type of trauma or loss. I believe this one line from that reporter about the Writebol family has a lot to teach us about the power of naming.

Obviously, theirs is a lovely commentary on faith. This couple stood in front of the world and spoke humbly, graciously, and with great hope about their experience. They held on to joy, and I'm sure that's the point the reporter was making when she said theirs was a "narrative of joy." What a beautiful testimony to the presence of God, that this couple who had been through so much could stand in front of the world and say in so many words, "This was hard, but our God is good and we trust him completely."

This was their public response, and it was good and appropriate. But it was just that: *their* response. When we're in the midst of difficult times, not everyone responds as the Writebols did, at least not at first. As people who put their trust in Jesus, sometimes we don't know what to say when we see someone going through an impossible time. Instead of giving them space to name their own narratives, we rush them into a narrative that makes us feel more comfortable. It can be easy to refuse to let people grieve the way they need to grieve by naming their circumstance for them, saying phrases like, "God is in control" or "Consider it all joy!" or "God works all things together for good."

He is, it is, and he does. But we are all on our own journey of living in to those truths. We would do well to create space for others to walk a little ways into that truth and begin to name their own narratives in time. We would do well to give ourselves that same space too.

When she said *theirs is a narrative of joy*, what the medical correspondent caught onto was the narrative, and a narrative implies a story. Theirs was a beautiful story of faith, but a story has an arc. That statement to the press was a plot point in the story. But it takes many plot points to make an arc.

The story arc can be one of hope even though each part of the story may have had its share of hopelessness. The story arc can be one of faith even though the characters may have shaken fists and asked hard questions and yelled at the top of their lungs. The story arc is joyful even when the people are broken.

I am thankful that the Writebols were able to go on national television and share their honest story that truly is a narrative of joy. I also want to remember, though, that within each narrative there are almost always shadows of gray along the way. And it's important to name those too. That's what makes it a narrative and not just a moment. That's what makes it a story and not just a plot point. That's what makes it a life.

We often don't give our narratives much thought. We just let time roll into itself, day after week after year. And then we realize, when we look back, that our story has changed. Our work today is to take a moment and notice the narrative, open it up in the presence of God, and allow him in to be with you, to gently confront the false beliefs if needed, and to provide you the peace of his presence.

○  ○  ○

If you feel stuck in a hopeless place today, I don't want to rush you to joy. Maybe you need to spend a little time letting the darkness do what darkness does—nourish, strengthen, and hold. The darkness can invite us into a mystery, a place where we don't know the answer. We know that seeds need to bury down deep in the ground, sometimes for a long, long time. Eventually, those seeds will break open and take root. But first they have to settle into the darkness. Still, that seed carries within it a narrative of hope. It just hasn't lived into the whole story yet.

Consider where you are in your own story. Are you at the beginning, in the middle, or toward the end?

If you are just starting out, are you afraid of looking like a fool? Are you worried they were right, and you're not cut out for this after all? This is not the whole story. Let today be a beginning, not a verdict.

Maybe you're in the middle, and discouragement or failure or just plain monotony stretch out both behind you and before you. This, too, is a plot point. Though it may be long, it isn't the whole arc. The middle still counts even though it's ordinary. Maybe the middle counts most of all.

You could be at an end of a season, a struggle, or some other kind of goodbye. Is this the ending you wanted? Is it the one you hoped it would be? Are you feeling disappointed? Nervous? Indifferent? Relieved?

Look at all these, then call them what they are. There is power in naming the unnamed things. This is an important part of our decision-making practice and key to taking our next right step in love. Remember today is a plot point. See it honestly for what it is, but don't confuse the moment for the whole story.

One final thing to remember: naming is not the same as explaining. A few months ago I was having back pain, so I went to get a massage and the therapist pointed out that the side I was having trouble with wasn't the side where she noticed the most tension. Immediately I went into question mode. "Well, what does that mean?! Is that bad?"

I wanted an answer, an explanation for what was happening with my back, and I thought maybe she had discovered it. But her answer taught me an important lesson.

"It's not bad," she said. "It's just information."

I wanted her not only to notice but to diagnose. But a name is more like a song than a definition. Sometimes the song is all you need. Other times, you play that song on repeat to let its melody smooth the jagged edges of your soul. If you take time to name something that has remained unnamed within you—a fear, a loneliness, a heartbreak, a dream, or a regret—resist the urge to grab and go. Instead, give that name some space to rise up and take shape. Then get curious about it. Hold it in the presence of Jesus. Ask him for direction and wisdom. Let yourself be a gatherer of information when it comes to what's happening beneath the surface. Name it, but don't force a definition.

## ○ A PRAYER

*Father, you hear everything, even the things we are afraid to say.*

*For all the ways we've experienced healing, we know there is still much within us that remains unseen and unnamed.*

*Give us the courage to face what we have so long tried to ignore.*

*Shine the warm light of grace into the shadows and be the courage we need to respond.*

*Hold shame, fear, and anger back with your powerful hand and extend to us your Father-kindness, we pray.*

*As we turn our face to you, may we see our true self reflected in your gaze, not as people who have a spirit of fear but one of power, love, and a sound mind.*

*Be our peace as we take one step forward and do our next right thing in love.*

*Remind us that, in Christ, we live a narrative of joy.*

## ○ A PRACTICE: NAME THE NARRATIVE

Here are questions that could help the unnamed realities rise up to the surface today:

Is there a hurt you haven't quite let go?

A regret that's been following you for so long you think it's normal?

An excitement you haven't given yourself permission to explore?

A dream that might be hanging out in the wings, kicking at rocks or standing on tiptoe?

Did one of your children just start kindergarten or go off to college?

Did you or your spouse start a new job?

Is there someone in your family with a recent diagnosis?

Is a friend celebrating a success you wish was yours?

Whatever your plot points are, name them for what they are—disappointment, grief, fear, excitement, envy, desire, exhaustion, or hope. Be willing to listen, even if you're afraid you won't like what you hear. Be assured you will never be listening alone. Remember not to force definitions but to carry these names into the presence of Jesus, in whose Name we find our hope.

# *four*
# PICTURE GOD

o o o

*Never believe anything bad about God.*

Dallas Willard[1]

We've established that decisions are hard, and we want to make good ones. We've laid the foundation for our simple, soulful practice: create space, embrace silence, recognize distractions, and begin to name what remains unnamed within us.

My first goal for this book is to help you have peace about the decisions you've already made and give you some direction about the ones causing you trouble. I want to help you create some space, name your narratives, and do your next right thing in love. But there's one giant, as-yet unspoken foundational conversation we need to have before we move forward: what we believe about God informs every aspect of our lives, including our decisions.

If I asked you what you believe about God, you might list some lovely, true things about him. If you asked me that question, I would say God is our Creator who is loving, good, gracious, and strong. I would say he is holy and righteous, and he takes great delight in us. I would mention something about him being mysterious but also knowable. He is Teacher, Shepherd, Friend, King, and Savior. I would tell you about the Trinity, about the love of God the Father, the compassion of the Son, and the presence of the Holy Spirit. I would mean it all, and I might even tear up.

But if you look closely at my life, if a mini version of you could crawl into my head, look out through my eyes, and see my choices filtered through what I believe about God, you might read a different story. Because there is almost always a gap between what we say we believe and what we actually believe. None of us are exempt.

If we believe God is mad at us, we will be afraid of making a wrong move for fear he will snap.

If we believe God is distant, we will feel alone and untethered in our decision-making.

If we believe God is a scolding parent, we may delegate decisions to someone else so we can avoid the consequences.

If we believe God is wimpy, we will think that maybe we can manipulate him into doing what we want.

If we believe God is indifferent, we may feel he probably doesn't care what happens one way or another.

If we believe God is like a carnival barker presenting three cups, we will feel cheated or duped when we assume he is forcing us to guess which one is hiding the right answer.

Do we believe God is like a puppeteer, a kind old grandfather, an abusive parent, an insecure friend, a greedy king, a manipulative mother, or a golden retriever?

In our mind, has he chosen a number between one and ten, waiting to see how close we'll get? Is he standing in the corner of the room with his arms crossed and eyebrows raised? Does he roll his eyes, turn his back, or slam the door when we make a bad decision?

In the last chapter, we explored the importance of naming what remains hidden within us about our lives and the stories our lives are telling. But we can't move forward unless we also confront the false narratives we have about God and allow him to tell us the truth.

Dallas Willard says we always live what we believe; we just don't always live what we *profess* we believe. I don't expect this short chapter to uncover all of our false narratives about

God. But at least now we have admitted they are there. These narratives will always inform our decisions.

I can't say how God will speak to you. But I can say with a fair amount of confidence how he won't.

He will not shame you into better behavior.

He will not trick you.

He will not tease you.

He will not laugh at you.

He will not terrorize you.

He does not pull rugs out from under you.

He does not drop the other shoe.

He does not pull fast ones.

He will not roll his eyes, throw up his hands, or turn his back on you.

God is your Shepherd; he provides what you need. He invites you to lie down in green pastures. He leads you beside quiet waters. He restores your soul. He leads you in paths of righteousness for the sake of his own name. Even when you walk through the valley of the shadow of death, you don't have to be afraid. He will provide comfort. He prepares a table for you and takes care of you, even when your enemies surround you. He anoints your head with oil and overflows your cup. He is good. He is loving. And he invites you to dwell in his house forever (Ps. 23).

o o o

My last two years as an undergraduate, I was a commuter student daily dreading the task of finding a decent parking space. As a result, I tried to arrive on campus almost a full hour before my classes started in order to ease the frustration of frantically circling campus for a space. To my great delight, I discovered a radio program hosted by author Elisabeth Elliot that helped me pass the time. The program was called *Gateway to Joy*, and it was broadcast daily from 11:15 to 11:30 a.m. Countless mornings, I sat in my car before class and listened to her open her show with these words: "You are loved with an everlasting love and underneath are the everlasting arms." At that time in my life, her daily assurance of God's everlasting love was a welcome mantra, one I embraced and repeated often.

Something else she quoted, both on her show and in some of her books, was a poem called "Do the Next Thing." Now that I'm writing this book, I've become curious about where that poem came from. It was always quoted as "anonymous," but a little digging has revealed the phrase comes from a book published in 1897 called *Ye Nexte Thynge* by Eleanor Amerman Sutphen. In the first pages of her book, she quotes this poem in its entirety, giving credit to its author, Mrs. George A. Paull. Here we are, 122 years later, still hanging on to this wise advice. As you continue to carry your decisions with you, and as you confront your own false narratives of God, use Mrs. Paull's poem as your prayer. Imagine God walking with you, issuing a kind invitation to release the burden of heavy decisions into his care.

## ○ A PRAYER

From an old English parsonage down by the sea
There came in the twilight a message to me;

Its quaint Saxon legend, deeply engraven,
Hath, it seems to me, teaching from heaven;
And through the hours the quiet words ring
Like a low inspiration: "Do the next thing."

Many a questioning, many a fear,
Many a doubt, hath its quieting here.
Moment by moment, let down from heaven,
Time, opportunity, and guidance are given.
Fear not tomorrows, child of the King;
Trust them with Jesus: Do the next thing.

Oh! He would have thee daily more free,
Knowing the might of thy royal degree,
Ever in waiting, glad for His call,
Tranquil in chastening, trusting through all.
Comings and goings no turmoil need bring;
His, all the future: do the next thing.

Do it immediately, do it with prayer;
Do it reliantly, casting all care;
Do it with reverence, tracing His hand
Who hath placed it before thee with earnest
    command.
Stayed on Omnipotence, safe 'neath His wing,
Leave all results, do the next thing.

Looking to Jesus, ever serener,
Working or suffering, be thy demeanor!
In the shade of His presence, the rest of His calm,
The light of His countenance live out thy psalm;
Strong in His faithfulness, praise Him and sing.
Then, as He beckons thee, do the next thing.

Mrs. George A. Paull

## ○ A PRACTICE: IMAGINE GOD

When you close your eyes and imagine God, what is the first thing you see?

Are there colors, shapes, or outlines?

Do you see a face, a hand, the curve of a shoulder?

What emotion rises up in you, if any?

What is the look on his face? What about yours?

Take some time to consider what you've come to believe about God. Then read Psalm 23 and see if your friend Jesus has anything to say to you today.

○   ○   ○

Now we move forward, armed with a little space for our soul to breathe, with some finally named narratives about our life and God. We're ready to begin doing our next right thing.

*five*

# LOOK FOR ARROWS

o   o   o

*Sometimes the circumstances at hand force us to be braver than we actually are, and so we knock on doors and ask for assistance. Sometimes not having any idea where we're going works out better than we could possibly have imagined.*

Ann Patchett, *What Now?*

We accept that in order to become good at something, practice is required. Our parents told us if we wanted to get better at piano, basketball, Monopoly, or math, we had to practice. It's the way of the world.

Why, then, when it comes to decision-making, do we think we ought to just *know*? We make better decisions by making decisions, not by thinking about making decisions. It takes practice, which is unfortunate, because unlike dancing or driving, we don't get rehearsals or simulations with decision-making. Every decision feels like a final exam on the first day of class. In my experience, three areas that present the most complicated decision-making moments are faith, vocation, and relationships. These take a little more time to consider what's happening beneath the surface, and the consequences of those decisions have more bearing on our lives. These are the decisions that may be weighing us down and continue to present the questions for which we keep not having answers.

God often gives a faint vision of things before they ever come to be. It's not a full form, more of a shadow, not focused or clear. It doesn't come with steps or money or sure things, but it does come with hope. And hope is what keeps you going in the fog. Instead of those black-and-white answers we tend to love so much, what if we began to look for arrows instead?

The year 2012 was a time in our family when not only did our questions not have answers but each question actually seemed to birth even more questions. During that time, I had some books to return to the library but had to go inside to return them because the outdoor book return slot was out of order. I didn't plan to walk out with a book that day. But once I was inside, it was only a few paces to the shelves, so I took a minute to browse the spines in one of my favorite sections.

The title on a small book caught my eye, maybe because it was stated in the form of a question—and because it was a question I had been carrying around for over a year by this point. The book was called *What Now?* by Ann Patchett. I picked it up and immediately knew I would check it out based on this quote in the inside flap:

> *What now?* is not just a panic-stricken question tossed out into a dark unknown. *What now?* can also be our joy. It is a declaration of possibility, of promise, of chance. It acknowledges that our future is open, that we may well do more than anyone expected of us, that at every point in our development we are still striving to grow.[1]

The book is pocket-sized, small enough to read in one sitting. It's actually a transcript of a commencement address Ann Patchett gave at Sarah Lawrence College. The title alone resonated with me that day because John and I were living in our own *What now?* kind of moment, preparing to leave his position at our church of six years (after a total of twelve years in youth ministry) to . . . well, that's just it. We didn't exactly know. We were looking for answers but what we got instead were arrows, and so we followed them. This is a story of where they led.

○  ○  ○

The first arrow was the arrow of grief. Not my favorite way to start a story, but there it is. After John's dad passed away during the summer of 2011, we knew things would never be the same for a lot of reasons, the main one being that John was broken open by grief. After the funeral, John went back to work pretty much immediately, back to routine, back to his regularly scheduled life. But his soul lingered with the grief, and it wasn't long before the disconnect between the pace of his life and the state of his soul began to show itself in the form of panic, sleepless nights, and intense fear. That was the fall of 2011. Unnamed narratives will reveal themselves one way or another. If we don't have the capacity to name them with our words, they will speak through our bodies.

Because of his difficulties keeping pace with the demands of his highly relational job as a youth pastor, the church gifted him a three-month leave to catch his breath and simply be a person. During those three months, he didn't check his email, meet with students, see coworkers, or see the parents of his students. He completely disconnected from the demands of work, even putting aside his smartphone, replacing it with an actual flip phone, the number for which was available to only a handful of people. This, I know, is a rare gift. We are ever grateful to our former church for allowing him this time. I share this part of the story with you just so you'll know it was about more than quitting a job. It was about coming alive. This transition has been for us slow, deep, and far-reaching.

Another arrow we had been following for actually quite some time, even before his dad got sick, was the arrow of desire. This, as it turns out, was surprisingly difficult for my husband. After years in youth ministry, we began to notice the parts of the job that brought him life (relationships, small group discipleship, connecting with students on a soul level, teaching deeper life concepts) and the parts that wore him out (traveling, games, programs, hype).

I would try to initiate dream talk, you know the kind: *If you could do anything regardless of income or location, what would it be?* While I was able to chatter away about moving to a big city or writing books together or traveling the country for a year with the kids, John was always more hesitant. Even in our hypothetical conversations, he was unable to take pretend risk. His mind simply wouldn't allow his heart to dream.

Logic and limits often get in the way of longing. And longing is key to our growth.

It's important to be able to answer the question *What do you really want?* It can also be scary, but it was only when John and I began to honestly explore the answer to that question in the presence of God that we started to get a hopeful vision for his vocation. But it didn't come the way we thought it would.

During those few months away from work, John traveled to attend a course in spiritual direction in Colorado Springs. We had made these plans a long time ago, not knowing that when the time came to attend, John would be in a place where he desperately needed some clarity. We were hopeful that his time there would bring some answers for his vocational direction. What actually happened surprised us both. God met John during that short time away, turned some things over, and woke some things up. This awakening didn't come like a glorious sunrise or a blooming flower. Instead, it arrived more like a summer storm: dark clouds, thick air, rolling thunder. Here is where we learned that desire often lives next door to grief inside the soul. Access the grief, and you wake up the longing as well.

Upon returning home, John was more aware as a husband and friend than I had ever seen him before. Watching this man wake up to himself was one of the great privileges of my life. It was powerful, sexy, and full of hope and possibility. While there was still a long road of healing ahead for him, now he seemed to have focus, not for his job but for his family; not only for himself but for me.

He wanted to be fully available as a husband and father in ways he had been previously closed off. Looking back, I remember telling people in the months following his return that it wasn't so much that John had changed but more that he became more fully himself.

This, remember, was during a time when we were looking for some vocational clarity. We kept not getting what we thought we wanted and were handed something we needed instead. We were looking for a good next step and a vision for whether he should stay in his current job as a youth pastor or move on to something else. Instead, all God offered was an arrow pointing from John to me and from me back to John. We wanted to know the way, and instead, God showed us each other. For the first time in our marriage, we began to cultivate a respectful curiosity for our mutual desire as a couple. And the only thing we knew for sure was we were to move toward one another.

And that was it.

The decision is rarely the point.

For months we continued to have honest conversations with each other, continued to say prayers in the dark, and continued to seek counsel from trusted mentors and friends. I'll share more about some of those details in a later chapter, but there came a point when the arrows finally led to an ending, and we knew it was time to move on from youth ministry even though we didn't know what was next.

The first six months after he left his job were dedicated to rest, recovery, and home. It was during those six months that my book *A Million Little Ways* released, so the timing was nice. He maintained our home rhythms while I worked, traveled some for the book, and began preliminary work on my next book.

We started to attend a small church, quietly getting to know a new community, adjusting to our new rhythm, relearning how to sit together on Sunday morning, which, if you've been married to a pastor for any amount of time, you know is a really big deal. We learned how to relate in a church where my husband wasn't on staff. Those six months turned into nearly a year before we actually had any clear indication of what the second half of John's career and ministry would look like. We walked through some hard days, some pretty hopeless what-are-we-even-doing kind of days where it seemed like the arrows led to nowhere. But we kept coming back to the promise of God, knowing he wouldn't leave us alone. Dallas Willard, in his book *The Divine Conspiracy*, says "the most important thing about you is not the things you achieve but the person you become."[2]

If we really believed that, our decisions might not feel so heavy. That difficult *what now* time of our lives helped us to learn the truth behind those words, truth that quick answers would never have given us. That time of waiting and listening and not knowing what was next helped us shape our character, become more connected as a couple, and become less afraid of the next *what now* season to come.

It's been almost seven years since that time of our lives. Looking back, it was maddening on some days; we just wanted clear answers and instead we got faint arrows—to desire, through grief, and finally to one another.

From where I sit today, with John working quietly in the center of his giftedness as the director of a local nonprofit where he offers soul care and discipleship for pastors, couples, and young men in our community, it's tempting to forget the uncertainty of the road that led us here. But if I could be so brave as to say it, the vocation is secondary for us. Yes, he wants to feel like he's contributing to society. Yes, he needs to provide for his family—we both do. But provision doesn't only mean money, and I know in fact you may be able to testify to that. You know that even with enough money you may still not feel provided for. Because provision also looks like support, like communication, like turning toward the people you love rather than away from them. Provision looks like staying in the room together when it would be easier to walk out.

If you have a big question mark hanging out in your soul, maybe one that has to do with faith, vocation, or relationships, perhaps your next right thing is to take a break from your frantic search for answers and look around for the arrows instead.

Listen to your personal desire or your mutual desire as a family or a couple, and refuse to be afraid of it.

Laugh.

Take a walk.

Make some plans.

Hold them loosely.

Take notes along the way.

And when you start to worry, don't do it behind a closed door.

Let someone in to sit with you without pushing them away.

Because next week, you may need to knock a door down for the sake of the ones you love, and you'll want to remember what it feels like to be on the other side.

When you catch a tiny glimpse of the future, be sure not to smother it with your own agenda. Let it breathe. Let it grow at a healthy pace. Admit it's both delightful and terrifying. As you take your next right step today, trust that God won't let you miss your own future. Follow the arrows.

## A PRAYER

*Father, we admit we want answers and there's nothing wrong with that.*

*But we can trip ourselves up when we hold clenched fists around our own agendas.*

*We are looking for a plan, but then you offer us your hand.*

*May it be enough today.*

*Grow in us hope where confusion used to live.*

*Grow in us courage where once there was fear.*

*While we have an awareness of our future, keep us here in this moment for the people we love.*

*Give us eyes to see the arrows.*

*Help us to trust our own hearts as we put our trust in you.*

## A PRACTICE: MOVE ON WITH YOUR DAY AS NORMAL

In his book *Hearing God*, Dallas Willard shares that when he asks something of God—for direction or clarity in some way—he states it simply in prayer and then devotes the next hour or so to "housework, gardening, driving about on errands or paying bills," things that keep his hands busy but his mind open.[3]

Today's practice is to share with your friend Jesus directly the question you've been carrying, and then move on with your day as normal. It could help to remember these words, also from Dallas Willard:

> I've learned not to worry about whether or not this is going to work. I know it does not have to work, but I am sure that it will work if God has something he really wants me to know or do. This is ultimately because I am sure of how great and good he is.[4]

As you simply do the next right thing in front of you—wash the dishes, write the email, read the chapter, have the conversation—pay attention not only to what's happening on the outside but to what is moving on the inside. Look for arrows, not just answers. If God has something to tell you, and you continue to place yourself before him, he won't let you miss it.

*six*

# BE A BEGINNER

○ ○ ○

*I am not an accredited interpreter of Scripture, but taking thought for the morrow is a waste of time, I believe, because all we can do to prepare rightly for tomorrow is to do the right thing today.*

Wendell Berry, *Our Only World*

During my senior year of college, I got a full-time job as a sign language interpreter at a local high school. This was a big deal, because part of our course work as interpreters in training was to complete at least a semester internship. This was a requirement whether or not we got paid for it. I was able to finish my senior year, satisfy my internship requirement, and earn money while doing it so I could pay my rent. Win-win-win.

Even though it was my full-time job, I was still a student, which meant I had to have a supervisor come and evaluate my performance from time to time. The first time she came, I was proud to have her there, to show her what I was capable of and the good work I was doing. At the end of the day, she handed me my evaluation form. She was kind and encouraging, and I felt pretty proud of myself. Her evaluation scores reflected that, and after she left, I scanned the page, past the numbers, past the check boxes and formalities because I wanted to see the comments she wrote at the bottom. What did she say without a form to guide her? What came spontaneously to her mind about me and my performance?

Quickly scanning her cursive writing at the bottom of that page, I was pleased to see she had good things to say, a few specific suggestions, and generally positive feedback. Then at the very end, she summarized all that with this statement: "Good work for a novice interpreter."

Well! I did not know what *novice* meant, but I couldn't wait to get home and look it up (this was before we had computers in our pockets). I imagined it meant something like "brilliant" or "impressive." By the time I got home, I had convinced myself she thought I was probably a prodigy, some kind of savant, definitely way ahead of my time. Never mind the fact that I didn't know what *novice* meant. My supervisor thought I was brilliant! What did it matter!?

When I arrived home to my apartment, I logged on to my computer and asked Jeeves "What does novice mean?" My heart sank at the answer. It meant "a person new to or inexperienced in a field or situation."

Blerg. She called me a *beginner*. The worst.

Obviously, this was not the worst—this was a compliment. She was saying, "For someone new to the field, she is doing very well!" But I liken this to how it felt after the twins were born and someone would say to me, "You look great for just having had two babies!" It was the qualifier that was maddening. Why couldn't I just look great, *period*? Why did I only look great for a person who just had twins?

As a new interpreter trying to find my way and establish my identity in the field, the shame of being a beginner was both heavy and invisible. I couldn't name it at the time, but that's what it was: it was shame. *Why was I only good for a beginner? Why couldn't I just be good, period?* I didn't like being called a beginner, even though that's exactly what I was. Maybe you can relate.

Once you take the time to get honest about where you are, one thing you might uncover is this: you are a beginner. There's nothing that insults our capable ego like realizing this. So what might be our next right step?

I want to make a distinction here because I think it's important and overlooked. When we talk about *new beginnings*, we usually frame the concept with words and phrases of hope, like springtime, flowers blooming, a new love, or a new start. On a hard day, we encourage ourselves with the knowledge that tomorrow is a new day! Joy will come in the morning. On January first, we say "Happy New Year!" Easter is the ultimate symbol of hope, new life, and resurrection. Hallelujah. New beginnings are usually welcome. But *being a beginner?* Not so much.

We want our circumstances to change, to start again, to be brand-new. But when they change, we often don't give ourselves permission to be new *within them*. Instead, we want to rush ahead to mastery. We think we ought to know how to navigate the newness, especially if it's something we wanted, something we prayed for, waited for, asked for, or planned.

A new beginning! Right on. But me, a beginner? No, thank you. I'm not sure where the shame of being a beginner originates. And maybe for you, this isn't an issue. I know for me, though, I don't like feeling like a beginner even when it's true.

In times of transition, being a beginner is a part of the stress. Plus, it can be confusing, especially when the new beginning is good. Maybe you got a new job or you started a new school. Way to go! But you don't know the ropes, you don't know the best bathroom to use, you don't know the protocol for things—or your computer password. You don't know the inside jokes or where people eat lunch. The list of what you don't know feels endless.

If you are newly engaged or newly pregnant, or if you are a new stepparent or just moved into a new house, you are grateful for the new role that you have and maybe you're excited about the future. But there's a lot you don't yet know, and there isn't a handbook to teach you. Maybe you are newly single or just divorced. You could be a recent empty nester or newly

widowed. To say these things are hard is a massive understate-
ment, an insult to the reality of your current situation.

All of these are new beginnings, some joyful and some
heartbreaking. But in all of these, you are a beginner. You
have not been here before, with this particular set of circumstances, with these particular people, at this particular time
in your one life.

All beginnings, no matter what they are, hold elements of
both joy *and* heartbreak. When we enter a new beginning,
we have generally also experienced some kind of ending that
comes with layered emotions and experiences of grief, transition, and letting go. Don't be afraid to be a beginner. Be relentlessly kind to yourself. What if this is your next right thing?

If you find yourself in a time of transition, whether it's something you've waited for or something that was put upon you
against your will, here you are now, new. Don't be afraid. Let
yourself be a beginner. What would that look like for you today?

Admitting those areas in your life where you are a beginner
is an important part of your decision-making process, because
otherwise you may find yourself making decisions in order to
avoid looking dumb or feeling foolish, or to save face. These
are terrible things to base your decisions on. Maybe today,
your next right thing is to stay quiet when your instinct wants
to speak out. It could mean asking a question rather than fak-
ing your way through. Maybe you are being invited to wait
until you have more information, to move even if it feels like
a risk, or to say those three words you don't feel comfortable
saying: "I don't know."

Whatever your next actual step is, the first one is simply to
accept your role as a beginner. This is a respectable, worthy
place to be. See if you can find a way to access the child you

still are on the inside. Though our bodies age, our souls stay young in so many ways—always looking to be loved, to be safe, and to be welcomed. Rather than becoming an expert, children are free to be curious. Children are able to sit down and let other people know things for a change. Children are able to observe, to watch, to make mistakes, and to learn new things. You are in Christ and your smallness is not a liability. Your smallness is a gift.

Remember Jesus is not only your King and your Friend, your Savior and your Shepherd. He is also the smartest man who ever lived. You may not know how to navigate this new beginning, but he does. With him by your side, you have everything you need.

Embrace this unique time of being a beginner. Let him teach you what is right, what to say, and how to think. There will come a time when this new beginning will not be new anymore, and you may not feel the need for him as you do now. So let this new role teach you what it has to teach you. Let it form you into the likeness of Christ. Let yourself be a beginner and receive all the gifts beginning has to give.

## ○ A PRAYER

*Oh God,*
   *We confess our longing to be the smartest person in the room.*
   *Reveal to us the true fear hiding beneath the surface.*
   *We are afraid of not having the answer.*
   *We are afraid of looking like a fool.*
   *We are afraid of being a beginner.*

*As we fall from the crumbling wall of our own reputation, status, and ability, we trust you are the solid ground beneath our tired feet.*

*As we face those who have doubted us the most, remind us how you stand in front of us, behind us, beside us, and within us.*

*When we look for courage elsewhere, remind us to turn to you instead.*

*You have all the gumption and moxie we could possibly need.*

*We accept our smallness in your presence.*

*Replace our shame with laughter and our doubt with love.*

*Teach us to begin again with joy.*


## ○ A PRACTICE: SAY "I DON'T KNOW (YET)"

Pay attention to the areas in your life where you are a beginner. They may be obvious, like some of those listed in this chapter. Or they may be more subtle. Here are a few possibilities:

- You have a child who is slowly morphing into a teenager before your eyes, and you've never had a teenager before.
- Your skin, hair, or digestive system is changing, and the way you care for yourself needs to change as well.
- The job you've had for years just transitioned to a new technology, and you have no idea how to use it.
- You and your spouse started eating healthier together—he lost a lot of weight fast, but you have stayed the same and have some feelings about it.

All of these are places where you are navigating a new beginning. Pay attention when you recognize something you don't know—what to say next, what to buy first, how to log in, or why your emotions are all over the place. Admit you don't know, whether to another person or privately to Jesus. Welcome him into these moments of being a beginner. He wants to be with you.

*seven*

# ASK THIS QUESTION BEFORE EVERY HARD DECISION

o   o   o

*It may look like the clouds are gathering for a storm, but I can rest because I have God's companionship and that is enough. Decisions aren't so harrowing—because I know the light dawns slowly but will come as needed.*

Jan Johnson, *When the Soul Listens*

In late September 1989, Hurricane Hugo slammed into the coast of South Carolina, costing over seventeen billion dollars in damage by the time the storm was over. I had just begun seventh grade, and we had only lived in South Carolina for about six months, having moved from our home in Iowa near the Mississippi River. As a Midwest girl, I understood the world of black funnel clouds and tornados running furiously over flatlands, but the size and scope of a windstorm over an ocean was a level of storm I had no context for at the time. In the days leading up to landfall, I studied the weather map on the nightly news, repeatedly asking my parents, "Are you sure we shouldn't leave the state, though? Staying here seems like a bad idea." It was the first time in my life that our regional weather map included a coastline and, even though we were over a hundred miles inland, it was the closest we had ever lived to the ocean. The reassurance my mom kept repeating was that people from the coast were coming to Columbia to take cover. Our city was a town of refuge, the place to which the evacuation route led. It was little comfort to me at the time, but looking back of course I know she was right.

We couldn't change or control the weather. All we could do was try to stay out of its way. That's an appropriate way to handle yourself in a storm: take cover and wait for it to pass over. But it's possible to live with the dread of a storm even when the sky is clear without a threat of rain. It's possible to take cover even when there's nothing to take cover from, except for a heavy idea or a recurring thought in the night. This is especially true when we have a difficult decision to make.

Sometimes we're afraid to move because we want to avoid an unwanted consequence. This is when our lives become marked by hiding from the potential storms of loneliness, failure, isolation, or invisibility. If we don't take cover, then we might be overcome. Here's how it's looked for me, and the one question I've learned to ask before every hard decision.

○　○　○

When our kids were little, I lived in fear a lot. I was afraid of them getting sick and it never ending. I was afraid of me getting sick and not being able to take care of them. I was afraid of making the wrong decisions about where we should live, how we should school our children, if John or I should take a job or not.

When my first book came out and speaking opportunities started to roll in, I said yes more than I wanted to because I was afraid of missing out on something. I also said no a few times because I was afraid I couldn't pull it off. Fear works both ways, keeping you from doing things you might want to do and convincing you that you have to do things you don't want to do.

But one decision in particular stands out in my mind, and it came to me via email the winter of 2011. That email was an invitation to travel as a writer with Compassion International to the Philippines to see the work Compassion was doing on behalf of children. When the invitation came in my inbox, the first thing I did was tear up, of course, and the second thing I did was look up the Philippines on a map, even though I was super sure it was right off the coast of Haiti.

Let me assure you, it is not.

I wish I could tell you I jumped at the opportunity to see the work of Compassion in this third-world country. I also wish I could tell you that my hesitancy to say yes was because of my life stage, as at the time our three kids were still in elementary school. I wish I could tell you it was because of my work schedule. I was in fact in the middle of writing not one but two books because I was crazy. I wish I could tell you I hesitated to say yes because the dates of the trip coincided with my husband's busiest time of year at work. Of course I was also hesitant to travel to a third-world country and see a kind of poverty I'd not yet borne witness to. Not only that, but John's dad was sick at the time, and we were uncertain what his condition would be when the time came for me to travel.

All of these things were true and could have been good reasons for saying no. But they were not the main reasons I hesitated. When it came down to it, my reasons for wanting to say no to this trip to the Philippines were exactly twofold, and I'm more than embarrassed to admit them.

Number one, I was afraid to fly.

Flying within the United States didn't bother me, in general. I even flew to Spain once. But this trip would be different. The sheer amount of airplane travel it would take to get from the East Coast of the United States of America to this little collection of islands in Southeast Asia, well let me just tell you, it was a lot of flying.

That was the first reason.

The second was this: I was afraid I would get sick in a foreign country.

Let me break this down for you people who are not afraid of getting sick. Getting sick in general was already a fear I carried with me at that time in my life. But getting sick in a foreign country? That was like the MVP of sick fears. If fear of getting sick was an actor, getting sick in a *foreign country* would win all of the Academy Awards. Getting sick in a foreign country felt like the actual worst thing that could happen.

I went around and around this decision. For one day, I pretended to say no in my mind. That didn't sit well. Then I pretended to say yes, and that didn't sit well either. There was a tugging, a pulling, an unsettledness either way. After two weeks of praying, discussing, seeking counsel, and general ridiculousness, I finally had a candid conversation with our trip leader, Shaun Groves. He said something to me on the phone that day that I have never forgotten, and it is the question I ask myself now before every single hard decision.

"There may be a lot of reasons for you to say no to this trip," he said. "But please, don't let fear be one of them."

That one line exposed the truth for me in that moment. I wasn't fully aware of it, but I was basing this decision on a storm I was imagining. In an attempt to avoid an unwanted consequence, I was allowing fear to push me around. Once I named the fear, it lost a lot of its power, and so I found the courage I needed to say yes.

A side note to that yes? I didn't feel sure of it until after I made the commitment. I think I was subconsciously waiting for a sense of peace and clarity before I decided, and it never came, not on the front end. It was only after the decision was made that I finally felt confident in it. I was all torn up about that decision, tossed here and there between yes and no. It wasn't until I finally got down to the root of the indecision that I was able to move—the root, in that case, was fear, plain and simple. Finally naming the fear helped me take my next right step, and I was able to move forward with a yes.

When it comes to hard decisions, I no longer wait two weeks to ask this question. I ask it at the first sign of hesitation.

*Am I being led by love or pushed by fear?* The answer to that question isn't always clear, but I continue to carry it with me into every difficult decision.

It's one thing to live through something hard—to, for example, get sick in a foreign country and live to tell about it. It would be appropriate to *mark* that moment, to admit this was difficult but we survived it. That would be a dark part in the story, but it wouldn't be the whole story.

It's another thing altogether to create a storm in our head and then make our decisions based on a possible scenario that hasn't even happened. That would be like naming the whole story as doomed before it had even begun. We can't prevent storms from coming, but we can decide not to invent our own.

## ○ A PRAYER

*Unbound by time or place or gravity, you go ahead of us into an unknown future.*

*You walk toward us with love in your eyes.*

*You stand beside us when we find ourselves in unsure places.*

*You sit next to us in silence and in joy.*

*You watch behind us to protect our minds from regret.*

*You live within us and lead from a quiet place.*

*When you speak with gentleness, we won't ignore you.*

*When you direct with nudges, we move with ease.*

*When you declare your love for us, we refuse to squirm away.*

*When you offer good gifts, we receive them with gratitude.*

*When you delay the answers, we wait with hope.*

*We resist the urge to sprint ahead in a hurry or lag behind in fear.*

*Let us keep company with you at a walking pace, moving forward together one step at a time.*

*Help us to know the difference between being pushed by fear and led by love.*

## ○ A PRACTICE: ASK THE QUESTION

If you are facing down a big decision in your life, perhaps your next right thing is to ask yourself the question, *In this decision, am I being pushed by fear or led by love?* That may offer all the insight you need to take your next right step. In the words of Shaun Groves, there might be a lot of good reasons to act or not to act, but don't let fear be one of them.

## *eight*

# KNOW WHAT
# YOU WANT MORE

o   o   o

*It would seem that Our Lord finds our desires not too strong, but too weak. We are half-hearted creatures, fooling about with drink and sex and ambition when infinite joy is offered us, like an ignorant child who wants to go on making mud pies in a slum because he cannot imagine what is meant by the offer of a holiday at the sea. We are far too easily pleased.*

C. S. Lewis, *The Weight of Glory*

It was a sad day when I learned they were no longer going to air new episodes of one of our favorite shows, *A Chef's Life*. But you can still find reruns of this delightful documentary-style show, which follows the life and work of award-winning chef Vivian Howard, a native of eastern North Carolina. With the Avett Brothers singing the opening theme song and the gorgeous North Carolina scenery, it's easily one of our favorite ways to spend thirty minutes on a weeknight. We watch as Vivian blends family, food, and storytelling in a way that honors people, tradition, and Southern cooking.

As *A Chef's Life* grew in popularity, so did her opportunities as a chef. We watched each season as she had to field more and more requests for catering, traveling, appearances, and special events. By the final season she couldn't even walk through the dining room of her own restaurant without being stopped by fans for photographs. It seemed like the thing she most wanted—to be a chef—also became the thing that began to take her away from her restaurant.

Vivian had a degree in English, and something else she always wanted to do was be a food writer. When she landed a book deal to write her first cookbook, she had to confront the reality that it was time to delegate a lot of her responsibility at the restaurant, because what she wanted more at that time was to write that book.

Knowing what she wanted was important, but knowing what she wanted *more* helped her to take her next right step. Still, her decisions didn't come without mess and complication. Because, oh yeah, her husband, Ben, was also her business partner, and together they had young twins, something she was constantly struggling to navigate and balance. She put the struggle out there, was honest about how hard it all was, and publicly admitted this was not a glamorous life. When her cookbook finally released in the fall of 2016, it hit the *New York Times* bestseller list, which of course brought even more attention and opportunity her way. Today she is not only an award-winning chef with several thriving restaurants but she's also a bestselling author.

While I love the peek behind the scenes of her kitchen, the beautiful presentations of food, and the simple and compelling interviews she has done with her neighbors, one of the most fascinating parts of the show for me personally is to watch as Vivian was consistently confronted with the question about what she really wanted at this time, in that circumstance. It's not talked about explicitly in the dialogue of the show, but over the course of the series, she seemed genuinely torn in discerning what she really wanted. Her own internal struggle with priorities was almost like an invisible character on the show. While it's admirable and exciting on one level, it's also a lot of pressure for one person to carry.

I realize these are all amazing, privileged opportunities—*Should I be an award-winning chef or a bestselling author?!* I know. But it serves as a great public example of the importance of knowing what you want *more*, because how we answer this question of desire determines what our next right step will be.

Make no mistake—denying your desire is also an answer, and that will determine your next step too. If you don't take the time to admit what you most long for, decisions will still need to be made. But instead of stepping forward in self-awareness, you'll base your decisions on other outward things like expectations, habit, or some other kind of external pressure.

Perhaps you have an important decision to make, maybe even one you would rather *not* make. Maybe it's a decision that has been forced upon you and it's serious and time-sensitive. Maybe you think considering what you really want is a nice luxury for some, but you have to be careful about all this desire business.

What does the Bible have to say about desire?

○  ○  ○

When reading in the Gospels, I've learned to pay close attention to Jesus, specifically what he says and does but, maybe more importantly, also what he *doesn't say* and *doesn't do*. The action of God in the person of Jesus is recorded for us in Scripture. We don't have to wonder what God would do if he were a person. He is a person, and here is what he did. And so, as we enter into Mark 10 and a pivotal moment in the life of a man named Bartimaeus, pay close attention to Jesus.

We meet Bartimaeus along the road from the city of Jericho. He was blind, he was a beggar, and he had no other hope. Jesus was leaving the city along with his disciples and a large crowd. This is not to be overlooked. Imagine walking outside, in the elements, with a bunch of people. There's conversation, a fair amount of dust, and the kind of chaos and activity that always comes when people move together from one place to another. As Jesus passed by on the noisy street, Bartimaeus called out as loud as he could, "Jesus, Son of David, have mercy on me!" (Mark 10:47 NIV).

Did Bartimaeus just happen to be there on the side of the Jericho road? Was that his regular spot for begging? Was his rounded back and tattered cloak a familiar sight to those who frequented that path? Or did Bartimaeus have to plan it, knowing Jesus would leave the city that way? Had he heard the stories that had circulated about the man, the Son of David, the son of Mary and Joseph, the Son of God?

Bartimaeus couldn't see, so he couldn't watch for Jesus from a distance, timing his call in a carefully choreographed effort. He must have depended upon the murmurs of the crowd around him, paid special attention to the main points, caught the runoff conversation meant for other people, and hoped for the best.

He called out in the air above him, hoping his voice would carry above the crowd, cut through the dust, and land in the heart of God. This cry was annoying and offensive to the people around him. They tried to keep him quiet, to shame him for using his voice and making such a vulnerable request in public. But even as they did, something shifted in the movement of the crowd.

Because Jesus stopped walking.

The crowd had no choice but to stop with him, no doubt looking around and wondering why. Jesus heard the cry of the blind man on the side of the road, the muffled voice in the midst of the active agenda of the traveling crowd. What had been a moving mission came to a full stop because Jesus's ear was sensitive to a person on the side of the road.

When he heard that cry, he told the people to call Bartimaeus near to him, and immediately their posture changed from shushing to ushering, urging Bartimaeus to stand up because Jesus was calling for him. The disciples traveling with Jesus most likely thought the goal that day was to get from one place to another. In that moment, in the way God always does, he made the side of the road center stage. He took what they thought was a footnote and made it a headline, a side-of-the-road detour in the upside-down kingdom of God. A small circle formed around Jesus and the blind man who was now on his feet, cloak thrown aside, standing in the presence of God.

In this encounter, pay close attention to what Jesus didn't do.

He didn't give Bartimaeus a Bible verse, a lesson, or a lecture. He didn't chastise him, shame him, or shake a divine finger in his general direction. He didn't talk to the crowd, make an example, tell a heartfelt story, or pray out loud. Instead, Jesus asked blind Bartimaeus a question: *What do you want me to do for you?*

In her book *Sacred Rhythms*, Ruth Haley Barton says this: "Jesus routinely asked people questions that helped them to get in touch with their desire and name it in his presence. . . . He often brought focus and clarity to his interactions with those who were spiritually hungry by asking them, 'What do you want? What do you want me to do for you?'"[1]

When Jesus asked this blind man that question, notice also what Bartimaeus didn't do.

He didn't wave away Jesus's question as impolite. He didn't turn it around and say, "Oh, no, Jesus, let's not talk about what I want. What do *you* think I should want?" He didn't point to the people in the crowd and say, "Well, never mind. They have much bigger needs than I do."

Jesus asked a simple question, and Bartimaeus stood there in all his vulnerability, in all his neediness, with desire all over his face, and offered a straightforward answer: "I want to regain my sight" (v. 51).

And that is exactly what happened.

We noticed what Jesus didn't do, but also notice what Jesus didn't ask. He didn't ask Bartimaeus, "What do you think? What do you believe? What do you think I want you to do?" . Jesus asked, *What do you want me to do for you?* It was a question of desire. When Bartimaeus answered, Jesus told him his faith had made him well. All we know about Bartimaeus is he was blind, he called out to Jesus, and he answered the question that was asked. Jesus called this an act of faith. I wonder if the same is true for us? I wonder if stating our desire in the presence of Jesus is actually an act of faith?

When admitting what we want, it's important to note that we often have to make decisions based on things that seem, on the surface at least, counter to our own desire, either because of finances, family obligations, or other important responsibilities. But if we look further in, these things may be desire-based too.

You may continue to show up at a job not because you necessarily want to be there but because your deepest desire is to provide for your family, and that is truly what you want. At the most basic level, this is still an issue of desire. You want to provide, and so you choose to show up even when it's hard. But here is perhaps the most important thing to remember as you begin to get honest about what you want: even if you don't get what you want, knowing what you want can still be a great gift.

Bartimaeus didn't say, "I have to regain my sight or else." He simply said that was what he wanted, and he left the next step to Jesus. Desire is only toxic when we demand our desires be satisfied on our terms and in our timing. Knowing what we want and getting what we want are not necessarily the same thing.

When it comes to decision-making, in my experience the best time to decide what you want is before a decision is even on the table. The second best time is when you are confronted with a decision but you haven't made that choice yet. And the third best time is after you make a decision and then realize you based your decision not on your deepest desire but on expectation, habit, pressure, or some other reason that had nothing to do with what you wanted. Some of the most memorable things I've learned in my life have happened as a result of saying yes to things I never really wanted in the first place. But admittedly, that is a painful way to learn.

In essence, knowing what you want is valuable in all stages of the decision-making process—before, during, and after. The sad thing is many of us move through our entire lives not knowing what we want before, during, *or* after a decision. As a result, we live our lives as a shadow of our true selves, not fully knowing who we are and, in turn, who God is in us.

Whether or not we get what we want isn't the point. Bartimaeus stated his desire without any knowledge of how things would turn out for him. Jesus asked what he wanted without a promise of fulfillment. What must Jesus's presence have communicated to Bartimaeus to give him the confidence to state his desire there, in front of all those people? What kindness was present in Jesus's voice, his phrasing, his slow attention? Without the benefit of seeing Jesus's face, Bartimaeus had to depend on his other senses in that encounter with Jesus. And so do we.

Honor your design and image-bearing identity enough to be honest about what you want most. Not for his sake, but for yours. In turn, here are three simple benefits you will discover when you take the time to name and know what you want in the presence of God.

**One, knowing what you want builds your confidence.**
The process of determining what you want more is actually
a gift to yourself. It means you've taken time to give your
inner voice a place at the table. You are allowed to take up
space in the room. Knowing what you want will help you
to own that.

**Two, knowing what you want is a gift to the people you
love.** It means in those areas where you have a choice, you
won't waste your time playing a game you don't really care to
win. It means you will be thoughtful about your yes and your
no; you won't overcommit yourself or your family to things
beyond your collective capacity to support. Every yes you say
affects every person who lives in your house. Knowing what
you want is an automatic filter to help you say yes to the
things you've already predecided matter, and to let the rest
fall gently away.

**Three, knowing what you want can help you let go in
peace.** In other words, knowing what you want can help you
more easily release the pain of not getting what you want. I
know this one feels counterintuitive, but hang with me.

What you want is what you want, whether you know it or
not. If something doesn't go your way, your plans don't work
out, or you experience a disappointment, the truth is you will
still feel the disappointment regardless, but if you know why
you're disappointed, the healing can come much more quickly.

I cannot tell you the number of times I've had to work
through layers of grief, anger, frustration, and fatigue after a
life experience only to realize later the real reason for all that
negativity was I had a particular desire I had not yet named.
When that desire went unmet, I felt it. *But I didn't know why.*
And so that disappointment came out in other weird ways

such as irritability, insecurity, lashing out, and silent treatments. It's remarkable the lengths my subconscious will go to in order to mask my truest desire.

Let's agree that knowing what we want is not the same as getting what we want, and certainly not the same as demanding what we want. When I honestly admit what I most long for *in the presence of Jesus*, I can more quickly accept when it doesn't work out. I can talk to him about it, admit my heartbreak, and receive what he has to give in place of it. This is what it means to walk with him in my everyday disappointment. There is no way to avoid it.

When I am honest with myself about what I most want, I must also confront the reality that what I most want I *may* not get. If you picked up this book because you desperately needed help with a particular decision or a series of decisions, chances are good that taking some time to admit what you most want could make the difference between a yes or a no, a now or a not yet, a here or a there. If not, though, remember these three benefits to knowing what you want: a newfound confidence, a deeper love and consideration for your people, and a willingness to let go.

○ **A PRAYER**

> *We don't want to be afraid of our own desires but to confess them in your presence.*
> *When our desires are fulfilled, remind us to be thankful.*
> *When our desires are unmet, remind us to keep hope.*
> *Help us to trust that because we've gained a new heart, our desires will lead us someplace good.*

*If we are unable to name our desires, when we feel
stuck, alone, and completely tapped out, help us to have
patience with ourselves and to believe you will tell us what
we need to know when we need to know it.*

○ A PRACTICE: **SAY WHAT YOU WANT MOST**

For the next twenty-four hours, practice pausing when someone asks your opinion on simple things, such as where to eat
lunch, which outfit looks better, or what the order of events
should be at the meeting, for example. Pausing is important
no matter if your personality is hesitant or assertive. If you're
hesitant, the pause could serve as a good reminder: *what you
want matters.* If you're traditionally more assertive and say
what you want quickly, the pause could help you discern what
you want *more.* This is a mini version of our decision-making
practice: create space, name the unnamed things, and do the
next right thing.

For today, that could look as simple as refusing to give your
usual *Oh, I don't care where we go, wherever you want!* or your
quick-to-take-charge *Let's do this!* response. Either way, the
pause will begin to create space for your daily decisions to be
more congruent with your inner life.

*nine*

# MAKE THE MOST
# IMPORTANT LIST

○　○　○

*Is the life you're living the same life that
wants to live in you? Before you tell your
life what you intend to do with it, listen for
what it intends to do with you.*

Parker J. Palmer, *Let Your Life Speak*

Generally, in our culture, we say something was the right decision if it was a success and the wrong decision if it was a failure. But what do success and failure really mean, and who gets to decide?

Life is filled with choices, and we make many of them without much thought. But when it comes to choosing between two equally good things (or worse, two equally awful things) how do we know when to say yes and when to say no? How can we reflect on past decisions in order to inform future ones, like where to live, where to work, how to school, or even what to make for dinner? From small choices with little consequence to big choices with great consequence, all of these decisions pull hard at our need to think clearly, to organize our thoughts, and to make the best possible choices with the information we have.

Here, in chapter 9, we're finally going to make a list. I've held off on purpose from leading you through a list-making practice thus far, mainly because lists tend to major on externals that, while important, are not our biggest determiner of making decisions, at least not on the simple, soulful path we're on together. So we'll do it a little differently than the way you may be used to. For example, one of the most common kinds of lists we make when considering a decision is the pro/con list.

I recently watched an episode of *Gilmore Girls* where Rory has to decide what college she wants to go to (for the fans, that's season 3, episode 17, "A Tale of Poes and Fire"). She makes three pro/con lists: one for Harvard, one for Princeton, and one for Yale. By making the lists, rule-follower that she is, she vows to obey them, whatever they may say. At the end of the episode, when she finally makes her decision (I will not give spoilers, even though it's been fourteen years since that episode aired), the camera zooms in to her pro/con list, showing the winning school to have more pros than cons.

My personal position on pro/con lists is that they are kind of dumb. I put them in the same category as key lime pie and pictures of bare feet on the internet. In other words, *No thank you.* I hold fast to that opinion on regular days and go about my business. Until, that is, I find myself in the position of having to decide between two great things, or two terrible things, or two equally-impossible-to-choose-from things. Once I'm staring down a huge decision and I just can't figure out what to do, it's easy to become that cliché that I hate, pull out a sheet of college-ruled paper, draw a line down the middle, and start organizing all thoughts and details into columns beneath plus and minus signs.

Some good things can emerge from a pro/con list. It can help you work out what you actually think. Writing things down in a methodical fashion has a way of clearing the mind, allowing you to make sense of something you might otherwise have trouble deciphering. But a pro/con list has at least one major flaw: it assumes every line item weighs an equal amount, and we all know they don't. A list could have ten cons on it and only one pro. But if that one pro is your family or your health or your safety, well, then that one item on the pro list outweighs all the items on the con list. Another major flaw with the pro/con list? We tend to make them only when we're feeling desperate, under the pressure of a deadline. Our final call on an important decision is fast approaching, and the pressure is mounting. Regardless of the outcome, I don't enjoy making hasty decisions. So why not make a different kind of list?

While it's not always possible to avoid making decisions under pressure, it *is* possible to give ourselves our best chance at lightening the load. My goal is to help you create space for your soul to breathe so you can discern your next right thing. Sometimes we have trouble knowing what to do next because we're in a season of busyness and hustle, and we just need someone to remind us to slow down and take a breath. Other times, though, we might be nearing the end of a season and looking ahead, and we need help to discern what our future steps might be. We need a way to make saying yes and no easier so that every single decision doesn't weigh so much.

The most important list to make is one that helps us to intentionally discern our yes and our no before the time comes to make the decision in the first place. I call that most important list a Life Energy List (one day I'm going to come up with a better name for it). This list is preemptive, not reactive. It won't eliminate your need to decide things when decisions come your way, but it could serve as a helpful filter for future decisions.

When we stand at the finish line of one season and the starting edge of the next, what we normally do is race into the next season without considering the one we just moved through. That's understandable, but it could also be costing us something, and we may not realize it until we approach that same season a year from now. This is a gift to your future self, an alternative to the pro/con list.

Take a few minutes to create a Life Energy List for the season you just experienced by intentionally looking back and asking yourself two questions:

What was life-draining?
What was life-giving?

97

It's simple, it's revealing, and here's how it works.

First, choose a category of your life. Second, choose a specific time frame, preferably no longer than one season of about three months. I've even chosen much shorter time frames, like a month or a few weeks. This helps keep things manageable. If you're already struggling with chronic hesitation or decision fatigue, you don't need me to tell you to look at the last ten years of your life and decide what was life-giving. That's too much time. Be specific and start small.

For example, let's say the category I choose to reflect on is *relationships* and the time frame I look at is *this past summer*. Things I will reflect on for this Life Energy List will be our community group activity for the summer, what volunteer commitments I did or did not engage in, time I spent with friends, date nights with John, daily life with family, time with other couples, and any traveling we might have done with other people. This may be the only category I have time for right now, and that's okay. You might be surprised what you learn when you take some time to reflect this specifically on your life.

Once you've spent some time reflecting on the category and time frame you chose, hold that season in your mind and ask yourself in each area if it felt life-draining or life-giving. Write your answers down on an actual list. I usually have my two lists on one page, with life-draining at the top and life-giving at the bottom (trust me, it's better to end with the life-giving stuff). When I did this for myself, I realized one of the things on my life-giving list was having a cookout with our extended family. But we only did that one time the whole summer. This helped me know what I might like to add more of to my life.

You can get as specific as you want and break down your categories into as much detail as you want. There is no wrong way to do this as long as you practice reflecting on your life and getting honest about the things that bring life and the things that drain life.

Some other categories you may choose to look at could include work, travel, church life, community involvement, meal planning, business partnerships, Sabbath practices, workshops attended (or skipped), movement and exercise, and prayer and reading habits. Again, my main advice is to choose one category and one specific time frame, and to always write it down.

Scan the areas of your life, choose one to reflect on, and then ask yourself, *Was this life-giving or life-draining?* Overall, when you think of it, does your body lift when you imagine that time or does it sink? Another way to ask the question, especially if you're looking at some of your spiritual disciplines, is this one: *Did this activity draw me closer to God or push me further from him?* Remember, there are no wrong answers. What is life-giving for me may be life-draining for you. Not only that, what is life-giving for you today may feel draining this time next year.

When we don't take time to reflect and reevaluate, then we may fall into the habit of doing things simply because they're what we've always done. We can't always eliminate the life-draining things, but that's not what this process is for. We will always have things we have to do in our lives, no matter how we feel about them. It's called being a grown-up. You will discover things on your life-draining list that you cannot remove or avoid. But the truth remains: we always have things in our life we say yes and no to based on knee-jerk reactions, expectations, or fears, and it's helpful to know what they are.

Another thing to notice is that there may be things on your list that feel life-draining, but the *result* of that thing is actually life-giving. For example, maybe it drains you to think of having people over to your house. Maybe you are an introvert and quite honestly would rather be alone. But you also value connection with people. As a result, having people over might show up on both lists for you. In fact, when you look back over your summer, having already been through it, it might seem as though that activity was life-giving. But next weekend when you have the opportunity to have people over it might feel life-draining. It may help to remember that while on the front end it might feel life-draining, what you'll remember is how much life it gave you in the end.

The Life Energy List is simply one tool to help you pay attention to your actual life so that you can discern what your next right thing might be. It helps you to listen to your life and let your past decisions inform future ones. You can make this list as often as is appropriate, from monthly to quarterly to maybe even yearly, but I suggest you do it a little more often than that.

What is life-giving? Your current life will give you hints; it always does. Your body gives you hints. Your mood gives you hints. Your family gives you hints. I never have to think twice or wonder. I always know as soon as I name them. You will too.

This is a practice in collecting the clues from your life and getting them down on paper so that when opportunities, commitments, and requests come your way in the future, you will be able to consider them with information from your actual life rather than frantic speculation and last-minute pro/con lists.

○   ○   ○

When I was invited to travel with Compassion to the Philippines, it was hard for me to know if I should say yes or no. I felt lost, untethered, and unsure. But if I had been in the practice of paying attention to what drained life and what gave life, I believe that decision would have come more quickly for me. I believe I would have been able to say yes sooner and with more confidence.

Does that mean if I had said no to that trip then I would have been wrong? I think that's actually the wrong question. Instead, I think it's important to realize that while sometimes there is a morally right or wrong decision, most of our daily decisions aren't so black and white.

Here's the truth: you can only make decisions based on what you know at the time. We live in an outcomes-based culture, where the correctness of our choice seems based on the success of the result. That might work in some situations, but is that really how we want to live our lives? Successful outcomes might look great on paper, but we want to build our lives on love, faith, connectedness, redemption, laughter, wholeheartedness, joy, and peace. Instead of asking which would be the exact right choice, consider the *life* choice. Jesus says he is the way, the truth, and the life. When we walk with him and consider his presence with us, then we can trust he will lead us toward life, so that even in the things that feel draining we can trust him as our life.

Making the most important list is a data-collecting practice, a process of becoming curious. You're waking up from the autopilot way of doing life. The last thing you want is for your Life Energy List to become just another way you put things on autopilot. *Well, I only do things that bring me life, so forget all of that other stuff.*

No, please no. This is all done in curiosity and with a listening posture. We make our list alongside Jesus and bring these things to him, asking him in every situation what he wants us to do. And then we trust that our desire can be trusted because he isn't just with us; he lives within us and he'll let us know what we need to know. We can get honest about how certain things bring us life and how other things don't. And then we listen.

While his character never changes, his leading might. What he led you to say no to last month may turn into a yes next month, regardless of its life-giving possibility. This is a relationship, not a spreadsheet; a rhythm, not a rule.

If you feel more like a robot with a to-do list in your hand than an artist with wonder in your eyes, stop. Close your eyes, open one hand in your lap and put the other on your heart, and ask yourself, *What am I longing for in this moment? What is life-giving?* If you do this, you might be surprised what you discover, but don't be surprised by the tears. Those tiny messengers are your kind companions, sent from the deepest part of who you are to remind you of what makes you come alive. Listen to them and wake up to your heartbeat. No matter the choice you make today or in the future, Jesus is with you. He has gone before you. And he will remain with you no matter the result.

○ **A PRAYER**

> *We admit we'd like to know the plan before we agree to it, but we're beginning to understand that's not really how you roll.*
>
> *As we take a little time to look back at our lives, give us the courage to admit what was hard and embrace what we love.*
>
> *Remind us to move toward life, again and again.*

*We ask today for a hopeful vision of the future even
while we sit with question marks.*

*Thank you for being with us and within us and for never
leaving us alone.*

## ○ A PRACTICE: MAKE THE MOST IMPORTANT LIST

You may already practice a similar reflection on a smaller
scale called the Daily Examen, which is a simple technique
of prayerful reflection you can engage in at the end of every
day. This is an ancient practice of looking back to discern
God's movement in your life that day and prayerfully paying
attention to how he might be directing you. This is one of my
favorite spiritual practices, and the Life Energy List is even
easier to engage in when I am in the practice of reflecting
daily. For now, choose a category and a time frame, and make
your own Life Energy List.

*ten*

# QUIT SOMETHING

○ ○ ○

*You can never get enough of what you don't really want.*

Rick Hanson, *Minimalism: A Documentary About the Important Things*

It was the biggest boat we had ever seen in the harbor, looming large over all the others. I had been coming to Hilton Head Island in South Carolina every summer for over ten years, and John had been coming all of his life. Still, this yacht was by far the most memorable either of us had ever seen there, making the other yachts around it look like toy boats run by pretend doll people.

As a habit, I confess I generally don't like to stare at impressive things such as cool cars on the road. It's exactly what they want us to do, so I always try to look the other way on purpose, my own quiet rebellion. But this time, I stood with everyone else, hands shielding my eyes from the setting sun, staring out into the harbor as that mini cruise ship moved slow, heavy, regal into the sound and then out to sea.

We overheard people say the crew had been dressed all in khakis and white fancy shirts earlier in the day, and now at dusk we saw them in their black ties carrying serving trays. Music and the hum of excited voices hovered over that boat in the harbor; an occasional communal roar of laughter burst through the summer night air as the yacht slowly made her way around the smaller boats. I nearly expected Jay Gatsby to walk right out onto the deck and nod to the crowd with a smirk and a white-coat wave.

As the yacht pulled away, we saw her name inscribed on the back—*Never Enough* it said, in gold letters. The irony was not lost on anyone watching.

Part of me wished I was there on that deck, surrounded by the buzz and glitz and mystery. What would it be like to not only be on that boat but to belong there? To be invited, at home among the glamorous, sun-kissed, and rich? But then, as I lazy-looped my arm through John's and we meandered our way back to our beach house, I realized that this life I live is someone else's boat. They look and long and wish for this. And so do I, until I remember I already have it. That glamorous life doesn't really exist, and the ones who chase it discover quickly, *It isn't really here.* Whoever named the boat knew that. All this stuff is never enough, not really.

It's been years since I first saw *Never Enough* floating slow and heavy in the harbor, but I still think about it. When I see a movie star on the cover of a magazine, I think about how her beauty and her money will never be enough. When I daydream about jumping on a plane to Paris, I remember trouble lives there too. When I look at women in my own industry who seem to have things figured out, I consider the *Never Enough*, how she may have been the biggest yacht in our harbor that night but she's not the biggest yacht in the world, not by far.

When you strive to be the biggest, the best, the smartest and wisest and most interesting, your goal will always be frustrated with bigger and better, smarter and wiser, and much more interesting. Rather than chasing *more*, what if we discovered *enough* right where we are? This is an important question to consider when making decisions, because for some of us, our yes and our no depend upon the degree to which we believe our choices will lead to the life we think we want—or worse, the one we've been taught to believe we *should* want, whether that be a summer night on a giant boat, a successful career, a white picket fence, and on and on.

Come with me on a short journey, one I bet you'll recognize, especially if you've ever spent a lot of time and energy on something and then been asked to let it go.

o   o   o

It's 2001, and I've been working as a sign language interpreter in a high school for two years now. I'm good at it. Sometimes Deaf people ask me if I'm Deaf when they see me sign. As an interpreter, this is the highest compliment. I have my degree in Educational Interpreting, but I want to get certified nationally. That is my highest goal. But our wedding is in a month, so the trip to Atlanta to take the exam will have to wait.

It's 2002, and the six-hour drive to Atlanta lingers in my back as I walk into the exam room. John and I have been married a year now, and this is actually my second trip here, as the first time I came I didn't pass the test. My expressive language is good, I know, but it's the receptive skills that trip me up, and I know this going in. I yawn and the examiner asks me if I'm tired. I tell her yes, but the truth is I yawn when I get nervous. She leaves the room after setting up the camera. I'm supposed to start signing as soon as I hear a voice. The tiny red light is blinding. I'm being taped, and I'm a nervous wreck who can't stop shaking. If you could travel to the past and ask me why I want to become a nationally certified sign language interpreter, in this moment, right before my test begins, I'm not sure I would be able to articulate why. All the best interpreters are nationally certified. Shouldn't I want to be the best?

Three months later, I get the letter in my mailbox, the familiar logo in the left-hand corner. I hesitate, wait for my stomach to return to its correct position, and put a finger through the hole between the paper and the adhesive. *Congratulations*, the letter says. So I've finally arrived. Now my degree, the studying, the money, and the scholarship are officially worth it. This paper is proof.

I don't feel any different.

It's 2003 and they tell me I can use a golf cart to get around campus if I need to. My boss hands me the keys, and I can't help but laugh. The twins aren't due for four more months, but I'm big. I'm really big. I already can't see my feet. My boss knows that the forty-hour work week is starting to take a toll on my body, especially since the university is big and some of the classes that I interpret in are far apart. I feel ridiculous, but I use that golf cart anyway and absolutely love it. My boss is kind to me, and I'm dreading the conversation I have to have with her soon. *I'm quitting.* It's time for me to be home for a while.

It's 2005 and the twins are both finally asleep at the same time. They'll be two years old soon. An interpreting agency called today, and I told them no for the third time this week. I need to earn more CEUs to keep my certification active, but that idea exhausts me. There's been a shift, something strong I can't shake, an invitation I can't fully decipher but one that's growing like a wave beneath the surface. I want to write.

Years later, after my first book is published and I'm working on my second, I get another letter in the mail.

*Dear Emily Freeman,*

*We regret to inform you that your RID record shows that you did not meet the CEU requirements for your certification cycle that ended December 31, 2011. Unfortunately, this means that we are required to revoke your certification.*

All my years of school, thousands of dollars, hundreds of hours of study, two trips to Atlanta for certification, years of earning continuing education credits, and several years of working as a professional interpreter, now finished. What does it mean when what was before you for so long is now behind you? What does it say about you, your commitments, your choices, and your identity when that thing you worked so hard for no longer seems like a good fit?

I cried a little when I read that letter. Saying no to interpreting didn't come all at once, but it did come. That gradual no led to an eventual yes to writing. That's one thing about an intentional no: it can open the door for a life-giving yes. When you focus on what's missing, it's hard to see what's there.

Just because things change doesn't mean you chose wrong in the first place.

Just because you're good at something doesn't mean you have to do it forever.

Today, perhaps your next right thing is to slow down long enough to see what's taking up space in your life, to stop looking around and to settle in and listen. If that feels hard, it could be that you're spinning around, looking for the next hundred things rather than the next one thing.

Become a soul minimalist again. Take time to name the narrative.

○  ○  ○

Maybe you need a reminder to release your pursuit of what is productive, profitable, impressive, or expected and instead consider this: *What is essential?* It's the kind of thing we tend to save for January, but maybe it's a good question any time of year.

Essentialism is not about how to get more things done, it's about how to get the right things done. It doesn't mean just doing less for the sake of less either. It is about making the wisest possible investment of your time and energy in order to operate at our highest point of contribution by doing only what is essential.[1]

If it feels hard for you to decide what is essential, here are three ways to clear the soul clutter and get back to the basics.

**One, be picky who you listen to.** We'll talk about this more in a later chapter, but if somebody's words, plans, or advice make you want to hyperventilate, take a hard pass. Breathe. Remember who you are. Repeat. It could be this exhausting advice is appealing to your false self. That's usually how it goes for me, anyway. The false self can never get enough. David Benner says, "Our calling is therefore the way of being that is both best for us and best for the world."[2] Be picky about who you listen to.

**Two, schedule a listening day.** This one will take some planning, but it's worth your time. Remember, you're already spending a lot of time and energy on things you suspect may not be essential. Let's harness that energy and redirect it for the purpose of prayerfully listening to the nudge of your own life and calling. The point of this day is not necessarily to make your decision but to remember who you are.

Even Jesus did not arrive on earth knowing who he was. He came as a baby, fully dependent. His parents had to teach him who he was, and then Jesus had to work it out with his Father. I realize this may be a strange thing to say, and maybe I'm treading on theological ground I know nothing about, but Scripture says everything Jesus did on earth was in total dependency on his Father. That includes knowing who he was.

For forty days in the wilderness, he was tempted to act outside of his identity and yet he remained faithful to the call to be himself. He had to battle the critics (and sometimes his own friends and family) who thought he should be someone different: a king, a prophet, a military leader. He had to accept the true will of his Father, to die on the cross only three years into his ministry.

What kept him moving forward was not success, ability, skill, or the consensus of the crowd. What kept him moving forward, what helped him to do his next right thing, was knowing that his Father was with him. And he could only remember that as he spent time alone with his Father. And so it goes for us. You need a time of remembering, of being, of knowing you are not alone. So schedule a listening day.

**Three, quit something.** It doesn't matter what it is. It doesn't have to be big. When you say no to something small, it could help to build your courage to say no to something bigger. Remember, it's not for the sake of saying no. It's so you can say yes to what really matters. It's not so you can get something you don't yet have (that leads to the never-enoughs). Instead it's so you can move from a sure place of who you already are. Sometimes saying no is your only gateway to the world of your most meaningful yes.

Just because you feel unsettled doesn't mean you're not a content person. It doesn't mean you're selfish or scattered or that you just need to be more thankful. It could mean that, I guess, but it doesn't automatically mean that. Maybe instead it means, as Adam McHugh says, that it's time to listen to your emotions rather than preach at them.[3] Maybe your life is trying to tell you something. Maybe it's time to clear out a little space to listen to what you already know: that it's time to make a change.

## ○ A PRAYER

*Father, we ask for clarity, but we understand that's not your highest priority.*

*Draw us close in our confusion, our doubt, and our questions.*

*May we not work so hard to get rid of those things.*

*Rather, may we let the questions and uncertainties pave the way to you.*

*Help us to know when to say yes and when to say no.*

*Give us the courage to quit when it's time.*

*We declare you are always enough.*

*We believe it. Help us in our unbelief.*

## ○ A PRACTICE: DECIDE IF IT'S TIME TO QUIT SOMETHING

Take a quiet moment and ask yourself this question: *Is now the time for me to quit something?* These questions and the passage of Scripture below might help.

Are you working hard toward something only to realize it isn't quite right anymore?

Has your heart changed on an issue but your mind hasn't gotten the memo?

Have you been tricked into believing that doing more and working harder will lead to finally having or being enough?

The wisest king who ever lived was Solomon, a man who literally had everything he could have ever wanted and still found it lacking. Take a few minutes and consider what he wrote in Ecclesiastes 3:

> There is a time for everything,
>  and a season for every activity under the heavens:
>
> a time to be born and a time to die,
> a time to plant and a time to uproot,
> a time to kill and a time to heal,
> a time to tear down and a time to build,
> a time to weep and a time to laugh,
> a time to mourn and a time to dance,
> a time to scatter stones and a time to gather them,
> a time to embrace and a time to refrain from
>  embracing,
> a time to search and a time to give up,
> a time to keep and a time to throw away,
> a time to tear and a time to mend,
> a time to be silent and a time to speak,
> a time to love and a time to hate,
> a time for war and a time for peace. (vv. 1–8 NIV)

*This is the Word of the Lord. Thanks be to God.*

*eleven*

# STAY IN TODAY

o  o  o

*Like many addicts, I had sensed a personal crash coming. For a decade and a half, I'd been a web obsessive, publishing blog posts multiple times a day, seven days a week.... Each morning began with a full immersion in the stream of internet consciousness and news, jumping from site to site, tweet to tweet, breaking news story to hottest take, scanning countless images and videos, catching up with multiple memes.... But I'd begun to fear that this new way of living was actually becoming a way of not-living.*

Andrew Sullivan, *I Used to Be a Human Being*

I've been in California for nearly twenty-four hours now. I couldn't keep my eyes open past 8:30 last night, and, of course, this morning I woke up hours before daylight. It's surprising how much of an impact a mere three-hour time difference has on a body. Pulling out my phone, I find a coffee shop in Monticeto that opens early. I take a shower and get full-out ready, and it isn't even 6:00 a.m.

Glad I rented a car for this trip, I make my way out of the retreat center where I'm staying. It was dark when I pulled in last night, and now, as I leave before sunrise, I still haven't seen what this place looks like. But it is nestled into the rocky hillside, and I can tell it's lovely. Nerves and curiosity push me onward, searching for coffee and people, something familiar around which to grab hold.

I know the general direction the coffee shop is in, so I'm not using my phone to navigate. I'm reminded at every turn that I'm on unfamiliar ground, fascinated by how the streets here have no curbs, so even main roads look like alleyways. And just as I start to mini-panic and curse the darkness of this eternal morning, I turn down one street and up another and, like magic, there at the top of a hill, I am suddenly in the presence of a wide-open space with nothing but dark blue morning and the golden glow of a distant sun making her way west.

No one is around. Just me, the palm trees, and the empty, fancy restaurants. I hear a faint rumble I can't place, wondering if it's thunder or a train in the distance. As I lower the driver's side window, I realize it's the ocean, crashing just beneath the road. For a moment, I sit there in a rented car, where Butterfly Lane meets Channel Drive, listening to the churning crash of waves against a West Coast beach. Both awesome and eerie in the darkness of early morning, the presence of an unnamed longing lingers in the air around me. Tears threaten. I turn left.

Shaking the moment away, I put the window up and head toward the coffee shop, finding the right streets more easily this time. I pull into the small town center, and it's the only shop open on the road, the warm glow of light and caffeine inside. Through the front windows I see two men sitting in jeans reading their newspapers. I park, I even get out, but I can't go in. That morning sky has set out to haunt me. I can tell from looking overhead that the sun is working her way farther up, and I realize I haven't yet got my fill. Looking back to my map, I retrace my route back to Channel Drive, and this time when I arrive, I park and get out.

Knowing John and the kids are all up and into the day back home, I can't help but think of California as a carefree latecomer, sleeping in on an eternal Saturday. *The whole country is already awake and your sun hasn't even come up yet! There is a lot of life happening just over those hills, you know.* California doesn't seem bothered one bit about it.

I stand here mingling among other morning people and stare over the railing at the water, gray-blue rocks in the distance, a teasing line of golden orange hovering just above them. A woman walks near to me and we face the water, watching together in polite, respectful quiet for a bit. Soon she strikes up a conversation and, having been traveling alone for over a day now, I don't really mind it. Turns out she grew up here and her life has borne witness to a countless number of sunrises and sunsets. This beach in Santa Barbara faces mostly south, so they get views of both the rising and setting sun. It may be one of the most beautiful places I've ever been.

We wait there together, she in her running clothes, me in my ready-for-the-day outfit, both holding our phones in hopes of capturing the morning sky. Others meander out as well: a man with two dogs running free, some bike riders, an older couple holding coffees. We stand, we watch, and we wait. The sun, she's in no hurry. She's been doing this every day since the beginning, and she will neither wait nor rush for anyone. If you're here, you see it. If you leave, you miss it. No pausing. No recording. No fast-forwarding through commercials. Just this moment rolling into the next, with changing hues you can only distinguish if you look away and then back again.

The runner I've been talking with, I learn her name is Jordan, and she's waiting to find out if she gets a job this week. She decides to continue with her run once we've waited past the time The Weather Channel app tells us the sun will rise. We realize the cloud cover probably means we won't see the sun and her fire this morning, only her watercolor influence.

I'll never see this runner again, but her life will go on, and she'll get her job and probably move to Amsterdam for a month and then go back to LA. And she and her white teeth will keep on seeing the sun come up three hours late every morning. I don't want to give up on seeing the actual sun, but I've been up for hours by now and I'm in desperate need of coffee. Returning to my rental car, I retrace my path and find The Coffee Bean and Tea Leaf again, but I cannot bring myself to get out of my car. What if the sun peeks through the clouds after all? What if I waited there by the water for thirty minutes only to miss the best part?

If you can actually believe it, I drive away again, head back to my old spot where I met Jordan a few minutes before, and again, the sun plays coy. With the sky fully awake, she has found a way to sneak up behind the clouds. This morning she'll hold her secrets close.

Resolved, I accept it's finally time for coffee and a bit of work. As I drive through the streets of the little town I'm coming to know by heart, I think about how ridiculous my morning has been so far, about how difficult it has been for me, since I got here, to settle in.

When we travel together, John always unpacks his suitcase within the first five minutes of arriving somewhere. When I saw him do this for the first time, I could not believe it. He doesn't understand those dressers aren't for using; they're for decoration and to put your stuff on top of.

I tend to look around, always wondering what's around that corner, what I'm missing, how I could enjoy this better. As I drive up to the coffee shop for the third time and finally get out of the car after chasing the sun all over Santa Barbara, I realize this one morning is so much like my actual life. I have a settling-in problem.

Psalm 46:10 is an invitation to be still and know he is God. There's a reason why God invites us to be still first: the stillness makes way for the knowing. It creates space in the same way becoming a soul minimalist makes way for the naming of unnamed things.

When I am constantly in motion, my body rehearses anxiety rather than practicing the unforced rhythms of grace. Ironically, in choosing to finally stop chasing something we don't think we have, we may end up finding what was always there.

Having an uncluttered soul isn't a one-time declarative statement but an ongoing way of being. Sometimes I feel centered in the early morning only to lose it by breakfast. Rather than being a scattered person unable to do anything, I want to be a gathered person equipped to do her next right thing in love.

The same way I moved between the beach and the coffee shop, I also travel between the past and the future, trying to avoid regret, working hard to predict outcomes, considering all the ways things could go wrong. I feel guilty about missing days with my kids in a summer that hasn't happened yet. I lose sleep over a conversation that I might have to have with an acquaintance. I imagine how someone might perceive me, and then I defend myself in my mind against that pretend perception. I allow my emotions to walk into the future without my rational mind, like a gang of toddlers without a parent. I can't possibly do the next right thing because I've traveled so far into the future that my next right thing is left behind in my imaginary past.

o   o   o

So, where do we go from here? Well, the only place we can go, the only place accessible to us. We go to *now*. Here's one simple thing I do to help me stay present to this day. And when I say it's simple, I really mean it.

First, take one thing on your mind that feels overwhelming, a thing that causes you to flit into the future and make imaginary plans or fret over potential worry. State what it is. Then turn it into a question and add *today* on the end.

Recently I practiced this before my girls started high school. While I wasn't exactly worried about it, it was something weighing on me in the back of my mind. I wondered if I was prepared, if they were prepared, if there were things I hadn't thought of that we needed to do. When I thought of it looming in the future, it felt overwhelming. For this simple exercise, I said, "I'm thinking about my girls starting high school in the fall."

Then I turned it into a question and added the word *today*. "Are my girls starting high school in the fall *today*?"

If the answer is no, you can set it aside. If the answer is yes, ask yourself, *What is the next right thing I can do right now as it relates to this concern?* If that feels confusing, or maybe it's so simple it's confusing, I'll give you another example.

Later this week, I'm traveling for a short overnight trip. It's kind of hanging over my head, and I'm feeling a bit scattered about it. So I state my concern: *I'm thinking about my trip to Raleigh.* Then I turn it into a question. "Is my trip to Raleigh happening *today*?"

No, but it is happening this week, and I do need to prepare for it.

*What is one next right step I can take today to prepare for this trip?*

I can't do it all, but I can do one thing. And then I can do one more thing after that.

What about you? What is something on your mind? Turn it into a question and add *today*. Sometimes the thing on your mind *is* happening today. The next question is still the same—*What is one next right thing you can do today?* Because that's all you can do anyway. You can only do one thing at a time.

○ **A PRAYER**

> O God, gather me now
> to be with you
> as you are with me.
>> Ted Loder[1]

○ **A PRACTICE: STAY IN TODAY**

Today we'll practice stopping on purpose so that we can, as Eugene Peterson says, "be alert and attentive and receptive to what God is doing in and for us, in and for others, on the way. We wait for our souls to catch up with our bodies."[2] If you feel scattered without a center, like you're flying out in all directions, let these few moments be a speed bump in your busy day. Resist the urge to scold yourself for being scattered. Remember that no one has ever been shamed into freedom. Let be what is in the presence of God. Acknowledge what is true. Say the day in your mind—the date, the month, the year. This is where you are; this moment is what you have. You can only be one place at a time. Stay in today.

*twelve*

# BE WHERE YOU ARE

o   o   o

*God meets us where we are, not where we pretend to be.*

Dr. Larry Crabb, *Real Church*

taying in *today* is an important practice for anyone, especially for those of us who may be more prone to anxiety and struggle with predicting worst-case scenarios. But there is another related practice that is equally important, and that is learning to be where you are. While staying in today keeps us from rushing into the future, being where we are allows us to admit what's really going on in the present. Several years ago, my failure to do this well eventually led to an important realization.

Sometimes our minds need time to process our realities, even when our reality is obvious to everyone else. No amount of lecturing or explaining will ever help us to see something until we're ready to see it for ourselves. That's why it's possible to be the last one to know that you're in love with that guy you've been hanging out with. And when you finally admit it, everyone in your life is like, *Duh, we've known that for months.* It's why when you finally admit it's time for you to quit your job or change majors or start something new, oftentimes the people in your life who know you best will just nod their head, relieved you've finally realized what they've known for quite some time. Several years ago, I was that person who didn't realize something that was obvious to everybody else. I still remember the moment it happened.

Walking home from taking my girls to our neighborhood school, I started going over in my mind all there was to do. Several things were normal house-things: I had to go to the grocery store, do the laundry, finish the dishes, call the tree guy, and price stuff for a yard sale we were having that weekend.

Other things were work-type things: I had to finish some photo edits, turn in something my publisher asked for, write an article, and prepare a blog post. As I approached my front door, I could feel my heartbeat start to speed up. My breathing became shallow and my craving for coffee shot through the roof. In short, I was stretched too thin but I didn't fully know why. About an hour later, while loading the dishwasher and planning out an email response in my head, I heard this phrase ping in my mind and everything came together: *Emily, you have a job.*

I know it sounds crazy to not know that, but when you work from home and you're also a mom, it's easy to believe the illusion for a long time that you are a stay-at-home mom. It was especially tricky because when I agreed to write a book and partner with a publisher, it didn't feel like a job the same way my past jobs did, since I didn't go to an office, meet with HR, or have to clock in or out. I didn't have workmates or a cubicle or paid time off. I didn't even have a boss, not really.

These aren't complaints; they're just to point out how gradual the change was. The lines between home and work were hard to see, and I was the one who had to draw them. At that time, I wasn't drawing them well simply because I didn't realize I needed to. The result for me was frustration, feeling overwhelmed, and the sense that I was trying to do everything but not doing any of it well. On a good day, I could only do most of it by half.

Admitting I had a job required a bit of grieving for me personally. Looking back, I never planned to start working at the time I did. But as I practiced the spiritual discipline of doing the next right thing, each of those next-right-things ended up leading to several book contracts. Those contracts have been a gift, and the income I've been able to generate mostly from home has blessed our family. But even good things come with shadows, and I'm learning to hold both the gifts as well as the burdens. For me, looking at the reality of my actual life and admitting I had a job was an obvious important first step that led to some much-needed freedom. After that, my conversations with John changed. The way I looked at our schedule changed. And, most importantly, I became kinder toward myself, realizing the only person who expected me to "do it all" was me.

This is an example of a time in my life where my situation changed slowly over time, but my expectations of myself didn't shift along with it. No matter your life stage or your circumstance, when things begin to change, it's important to be where you are and remain vigilant about the expectations you might be carrying around.

Do you see the power of naming things? My reality was one of a work-from-home mom but my perception of myself was as a stay-at-home mom. No wonder I always felt behind. When we don't admit or become aware of our current life situation, we will continue to have expectations of ourselves and of other people as if things are as they've always been when, in fact, they are not. When we're unaware of where we are, we can't possibly make informed decisions about where we want to go. This leads to an inability to discern our next right thing.

In order to be where you are, you have to *know* where you are. Let's engage in a simple practice to help you be where you are and allow God to meet you there. Here are a series of questions to ask as a way of naming what is true. Answer them without judgment, condemnation, anger, blame, or shame. That's an important part of this practice. Sometimes we need someone to remind us to simply be with what's true without trying to change it, fix it, or put a spin on it to make it sound better or worse.

Here we go.

Have you recently started a new position, been given more responsibility at work, or been passed over for someone else?

Have you had an injury or a sickness that has changed your energy level or ability in some way?

Are you having work done in your house for renovation or upkeep, and has this brought extra people into your home at odd times?

Does someone close to you need you more now than they have in the past?

Is a child or a loved one struggling with anxiety? Sickness? Heartbreak? Pain?

Are you waiting for results that are out of your control? How long have you been waiting for those results?

In general, have you added something new to your schedule without taking anything away?

Has something that was life-giving for you been removed from your schedule in order to make room for something necessary but maybe not as life-giving?

If these questions are hard to answer, consider asking someone close to you to answer them on your behalf. Maybe they will see something you're unable to see for yourself. Take all of these things you've named, or you've asked someone else to name for you, and sit with them for a moment. If you had trouble answering any or all of these questions, then that is where you are today. And there is no shame in that.

## ○ A PRAYER

*Father, help us to know where we are and then help us to be where we are.*

*Meet us in our weakness, our smallness, our exhaustion, our insecurity, and our questions.*

*As we move forward in the midst of where we are, help us to believe you even though we can't see you.*

*May we not demand a spectacle, a miracle, or a sign. May we simply, quietly, be still and know.*

*Even if we may be busy on the outside, don't let hurry overwhelm us on the inside.*

*Remind us to move at a walking pace.*

*Let your peace rule within us.*

*Quiet us in the midst of the chaos.*

*Lord, in your mercy, hear our prayer.*

## ○ A PRACTICE: TAKE A WALK ALONE

At some point this week, find fifteen minutes to take a walk alone. Preferably outside, but there's no wrong here. Whether you live on a busy city street, in a neighborhood filled with kids, or on a quiet country lane, a fifteen-minute walk can do your soul a lot of good.

There are no rules for this, but here are a few suggestions as you practice moving at a walking pace. First, walk without an agenda. Don't expect to come back from a short walk with new perspective, magic peace, answers, or a plan.

Second, leave your earbuds behind. It can be good to walk slowly and listen to the world around you rather than letting music or a podcast carry you somewhere else. Let the rhythm of your feet on pavement or grass or gravel pound out a melody of peace. Let the neighborhood noises preach the sermon for once. Listen for what you can hear: a distant car, a singing bird, a barking dog, an airplane overhead. Give yourself the gift of being with what is, all the ordinary sounds of this, your everyday space.

Finally, as you pay attention to your surroundings, what do you see and hear within you?

## *thirteen*
# DON'T RUSH CLARITY

o  o  o

*God's ideas are not always obvious, and are always more clever than we can imagine. Even though the circumstances may be the same as many times before, God may have a different and better idea. So we are wise to ask for guidance each time.*

Jan Johnson, *When the Soul Listens*

It's been ten years since we moved into our current house, but I still remember the pink walls with purple trim in the master bedroom and the living room walls covered from floor to ceiling with mirrors. Basically, we bought the house (even though Carol Brady herself would have called it dated) because we had a vision for what it could be. For several months we owned it but hadn't moved in yet because we had renovations to finish. The twins were four at that time and their baby brother was not yet two, and during those months of renovation, I would drive across town to the new house in the early morning hours before the kids woke up, leaving them asleep while John drank his morning coffee before work. "I won't be long," I'd say, and I'd pull into the driveway and walk to the back of the empty house, warm sunbeams of sawdust lighting the sunroom up with hope. Leaning against the doorjamb in one of the upstairs bedrooms, I loved the way the light lay in long lines on the hardwood floor. I could imagine that floor littered with colorful plastic toys, soft loveys, and board books. The walls weren't even painted yet, and the house wasn't near finished. But I could still see it even though I couldn't yet *see it*.

For the last several years, I've had some ideas for a few projects, both personal and work-related. Like the house, I can see them even though I can't yet see them. Some I've made progress on, and others I can't quite move on yet. But there is one particular idea I have that I haven't yet picked up. It's not for lack of motivation or conviction that the thing ought to be done. Rather I've had this unequivocal sense that I need to wait, like a hand is stretched out in front of me. The image isn't one of a police officer saying *Stop, you aren't allowed to go yet.* It's more like one of a mom who hits the brakes too hard and instinctively stretches her arm across the passenger seat. Kind of like that, but less frantic. More gentle. It's clear I'm to wait. It's not clear as to why.

I've walked through all the familiar stages of new project things with this idea—talking, praying, brainstorming, writing down notes and ideas, paying attention to the world around me and the world within me as it relates to the subject. But progress doesn't seem to come. Sometimes I wonder, *Am I just being lazy? Am I putting something off and procrastinating? Am I scared? Intimidated? Do I just not know how to begin this one?* That's when the doubting starts to come in, the wondering if maybe this project isn't to be done after all; maybe I have it all wrong or partially wrong or wrong enough to keep me from moving on it. When next steps are unclear, doubt is often the most logical conclusion. *Maybe I don't know how to hear God's voice after all. Maybe all this is just my idea alone.*

Many times we're looking for guidance somewhere out there, a sign, a word, an encouragement, a conversation. God speaks to us through the Bible, in prayer, and often through other people, but another regular way I know he speaks to me is the one way I have most often dismissed: through the voice that comes from within. The good news is I'm finally learning to trust that voice.

We can start down that road of doubt and questioning if we want to. But just because the doubts show up doesn't mean you have to let them sit down. They won't linger if they're not welcome. Instead, when it comes to those unwelcome thoughts of doubt and discouragement, how about let's point them to the door.

Let's make room for new thoughts to inhabit our minds, thoughts of courage, hope, and belief. I'm learning that still, small voice isn't the voice of age or wisdom or confidence. Those come as a result of listening to the voice, to be sure. But they, themselves, are not the source.

God often speaks in such a regular and familiar way that it's almost too normal to point out. We look for fireworks or signals or confirmation from somewhere other than us, thinking his direction can't possibly come from us. But he keeps on reminding us that he has made our heart his home, and that's often the place from which he'll make his voice heard.

○  ○  ○

If you feel distracted and overwhelmed by a particular decision and feel unable to think clearly about it, it's tempting to think something is wrong with your process or that something is wrong with *you*. Here are two things you can release that could help you take your next right step.

**One, let go of your timeline.** One of my favorite lines of advice about decision-making comes from Marie Forleo, who points out that clarity cannot be rushed.[1] It could be you're anxious to make a decision, not because it's necessary right now but simply because it's nagging. This is legitimate, understandable, and completely makes sense. But in order to give yourself the space to receive clarity, maybe you need to let go of the expectation that clarity will come in a particular way or at a particular time. This could be difficult, especially if you're not used to holding so much in your heart all at once without being able to move on it.

Much of the rhetoric around our work and life is that if you have an idea but aren't acting on it, then it means you're nursing some brand of fear, insecurity, or immaturity. The advice surrounding this subject says you just need to put your head down, drink more coffee, and get to work! But what about the work that grows slowly?

What about the ideas that take years to form?
The ministry that needs darkness and time to bury its roots down deep into you?
The book that only wants to drip out of you, one slow word at a time?
The business that requires an unrushed foundation?
Is the vision strong enough to carry your soul through the foggy right-now?
If it's not, are you willing to listen to the still, small voice and believe it's telling the truth?

Can you hold on to your faith while you wait? If it isn't yet time to make a decision or to move, practice the daily letting go of your timeline. But maybe that isn't the problem. Maybe the time *has* come. That leads us to my second suggestion.

**Two, let go of your expectation of certainty**. I mentioned Marie Forleo before, and I fully believe she's right: *clarity cannot be rushed*. We must be *patient*. But, paradoxically, do you know what else she says? "Clarity comes from engagement, not thought. When you take action, you'll access your natural knowing."[2] We must *act*. As you listen to your life and the Spirit's heartbeat, the vision will grow as the work is done. You'll begin to see it even though you can't yet see it.

Proverbs 20:27 says, "The spirit of man is the candle of the LORD, searching all the inward parts of the belly" (KJV). If you think about holding a candle in your hands, you know that if you walk too fast, the flame will blink right out. You have to take slow, measured steps, maybe even block the candle from the wind as you go. So, for now, walk slowly with the flame still lit and continue to ask your friend Jesus about the next step. If he lives within you, then that means he speaks, even now, through his Word, his people, and your own deepest desires as you confess them in his presence. Trust the voice that comes from within. If there's a longing or a vision growing within you, or if you have an idea, a project, or work you can see even though you can't see it, *carry on*. Walk slowly. Listen closely. And let that candle burn.

We've lived in our house almost ten years now; we've built our lives within its painted walls, and all my visions have become our reality. Once the renovations were over, that bedroom floor went from being cluttered with colorful plastic toys to Barbie dolls to Hot Wheels to nail polish and now it's drumsticks and volleyballs and a thousand mismatched pairs of Nike elite basketball socks. It's a slow work, building a life. But the future always comes.

## ○ A PRAYER

Read Psalm 37:23–26 as a prayer:

> The steps of a man are established by the LORD,
> And He delights in his way.
> When he falls, he will not be hurled headlong,
> Because the LORD is the One who holds his hand.
>
> I have been young and now I am old,
> Yet I have not seen the righteous forsaken

Or his descendants begging bread.
All day long he is gracious and lends,
And his descendants are a blessing.

*This is the Word of the Lord. Thanks be to God.*

## ○ A PRACTICE: LET GO

If you've been searching for clarity that isn't coming, is it time to let go of your timeline? Is this decision necessary to make right now, or are you able to wait?

If it is time to make the decision, let go of your expectation of certainty. You may need to take one next right step before you feel ready. Ask God for guidance and then trust him as you act. Be assured as you move forward that he is with you and continue to talk with him in each new step.

# *fourteen*
# STOP COLLECTING GURUS

○ ○ ○

*The love of Jesus will give you an ever-clearer vision of your call. . . . The more you are called to speak for God's love, the more you will need to deepen the knowledge of that love in your own heart. The farther the outward journey takes you, the deeper the inward journey must be.*

Henri Nouwen, *The Inner Voice of Love*

My decision fatigue was at an all-time high the day I sat down to clean out my email inbox. It felt like the one thing I had some control over. In no time, I realized that my inbox was telling me a story, hiding an unexpected source of stress. Finally, I slowed down long enough to listen. I wonder if your inbox is telling you this story too. Here's mine.

As I sifted through both the read and unread message boxes, a pattern began to emerge. I had emails from an Instagram teacher, a business coach, a book launch guy, a course creation lady, and a declutter-my-house guide. I had results and follow-up results from tests and quizzes that I took throughout the year about my personality type, my hair type, my marketing type, and my dressing type.

I love the online space if for no other reason than we can learn anything we want whenever we want to learn it. I am a huge fan of online courses and teaching. The courses I've taken have helped me reshape my own business and ministry, and the ones I've taught have brought in valuable revenue for my family, not to mention the deep sense of satisfaction and personal fulfillment I get from creating the kind of work that I feel called to create and interacting with people who can benefit from it.

I've also gained important insight about myself from various personal assessments. I now buy different kinds of clothes that actually fit my body better because of a course I took to help me learn about that. I have learned priceless information about book launching, marketing, decluttering, and a thousand other things. The material these teachers brought into my life was and is valuable and worth it.

But when I sat down to clean out my inbox that afternoon, I realized that over the course of 2016, I had started to collect gurus. All of these experts arrived in my life (or I sought them out) at a time when I thought I could use what they had to offer. As I combed through my inbox, past all of the advice and instruction, results and evaluation tools, I noticed my breathing became more shallow and my head started to ache. The problem wasn't the courses, or the email series, or the updates. The problem was I had too many going at once. I was trying to listen to way too many of those voices at the same time.

My work, what I feel called to and get paid for, is to help you create space for your soul to breathe. But making a living is nothing if I'm not also making a life. One thing I've discovered that helps me live my life more fully is to take inventory when anxiety shows up. Rather than avoid it, as I'm prone to do, I choose instead the simple, soulful practice this book is based upon: get still and quiet, create a little space for the soul, ask God what he needs me to know, and finally name what has yet to have a name. In this case, I needed to name the story my inbox was telling me. When I did these simple things, it was obvious I had way too many gurus talking to me. It was not as obvious as to why.

I took some time to ask myself that question, and as I did, my answer came simply and without hesitation. At that particular time in my life, I was looking for some clarity in specific areas, and I hoped one of these trainings would help me find it. I wanted help to clarify what continued to feel like a foggy vision for the future. This is somewhat of a predictable pattern for me. When I'm feeling insecure or aimless, it's easy for me to latch on to someone else's security and confidence, hoping that some of their clarity will rub off on me. As it turns out, the best time to look for an expert is not when you need vision, it's when you need a plan. It's a great idea to find teachers and mentors. You just have to do things in the right order.

When I start looking for help before I've established a clear vision, it leads to me feeling anxious, overwhelmed, and emotionally whiplashed. If I don't have a vision, purpose, or intention, then how do I know which steps are right for me to take?

○ ○ ○

Evidence of your own guru collection may show up in spaces other than your inbox. Maybe it's the websites you visit, the books you read, the podcasts you subscribe to, or the actual real-life people you pursue. All of these have value, bring encouragement, and offer company, perspective, entertainment, or education in some way. Again, the issue may not be about the teachers themselves but about their timing in your own life.

There may be some spaces, online or otherwise, that traditionally encourage you, but when you are working on a particular project or going through a difficult breakup or grieving the loss of a parent or whatever the case might be, the places that are historically good for you could become, for a time, not good for you. It's important to get honest about that. Here are some examples of what that might look like.

There may be a certain artist, author, or someone whom you follow who does work or has a life similar to yours, and normally you love to read her feed and like her posts, and you are encouraged there. But while you are wrestling with a decision in this particular season of your life, you may need to intentionally ignore that space in order to get your own work done, whether that is work you are doing for an actual job or work you are doing on the level of your soul.

This may mean you mute her feed or even unfollow her for a time. This doesn't mean you are being immature or petty. You could do this for a thousand different reasons. It doesn't mean you don't like the person, that you no longer admire her, or that it's forever. You just need some help discerning your next right thing, and this feed, this profile, these updates are not helping you do that.

You know yourself better than anyone else. And maybe your next right thing is simply to step away (even temporarily) from photos, headlines, images, or updates that cause anxiety in your life. But this goes both ways. Bear in mind that, at some point, you may be the guru someone needs to ignore. Try not to take it personally.

When we feel unsure, indecisive, or doubtful, sometimes we're tempted to look around and call it "research." For me, that nearly always leads to some form of exaggeration. It keeps me from being able to clearly discern my next right thing. I exaggerate other people's skills, other people's successes, other people's schedules. When I'm in that place it's easy for me to believe the myth that everyone else is winning all the time. I know it's not true because I'm a grown-up, but my body still responds with anxiety even when I will it not to. I feel behind in a race I might not even want to run in, much less win.

As John often says, "Pay attention to what you pay attention to." As you do that, you may notice the way your body responds to a tone certain people have or the photos they always share. Instead of paying attention to their agenda, pay attention to how you're paying attention to their agenda—hold it in your hand and consider if it's causing you some anxiety in your life. If yes, you know what to do.

We need to choose gurus or teachers or mentors who will offer plans that line up with the vision we already have for our life, our work, and our ministry. If you don't know where you're going, specific directions won't really help, not until you see the big picture. If you feel frustrated and pulled in many directions like I have felt, it could be because you've been looking for advice about the journey even before you know or understand your hoped-for destination.

If you've been frantically searching outside of yourself for help with a plan but you feel untethered and directionless, maybe what you really need is to quiet down inside yourself and listen for a vision. Vision and purpose have to come from the quiet place within us first. Only then can we seek insight for the next right step to take that will align with our vision. That's not to say that we are going to see a clear plan for our life laid out before we can know our next right step. That's the whole purpose of just doing the next thing. But too often, I take it to the other extreme and look for outside voices to tell me what can only come from within.

That very weekend, after the inbox discovery, I took my own advice. I got quiet. I took a walk. I stopped trying to wrestle clarity to the ground. I accepted the invitation to keep company with Jesus, not for the sake of a plan but for the pleasure of his presence.

The natural result of being with him is I remember who I am. I remember how my Father is very fond of me and will be with me no matter what. I'm grateful for the vision we continue to uncover together, and I feel more prepared to find the gurus, mentors, and teachers I'll need to help me craft a plan that makes sense.

## ○ A PRAYER

*As we grasp for answers, be our One Sure Thing.*
*We trust you as our Teacher.*
*Reveal to us the story our inboxes, mailboxes, bookshelves, and journals are trying to tell us.*
*Help us pay attention to what we pay attention to.*
*In your presence, we are safe to see and tell the truth.*
*Show us where we are frantically grasping for guidance and replace the darkened pathway with your light, the foggy future with your peace, and our longing for security with your confidence.*
*Bring to us the mentors and teachers we need for the journey.*
*May we have the wisdom to trust our own inner voice as we are united with you in love.*

## ○ A PRACTICE: PURGE YOUR INBOX, MAILBOX, AND/OR BOOKSHELF

Make an appointment with your email inbox or, if it makes more sense, with your work desk, your bookshelf, your calendar, or your social accounts. Your job is to pay attention without judgment. Resist the urge to draw a conclusion at first. Just let yourself notice and be curious about the story these things are telling you. These gurus, teachers, and mentors may have wonderful things to teach you. The assignment is not to get rid of them. Not yet. Instead, the assignment is to discern if now is the time for them. It might be helpful to consider:

- What is coming up in your life in the next ninety days?
- What can you reasonably prioritize in that amount of time?
- What practical help do you need for the journey?

*fifteen*

# GATHER CO-LISTENERS

o  o  o

*It is God's love for us that he not only gives us his word but also lends us his ear. So it is his work that we do for our brother when we learn to listen to him. Christians, especially ministers, so often think they must always contribute something when they are in the company of others, that this is the one service they have to render. They forget that listening can be a greater service than speaking.*

Dietrich Bonhoeffer, *Life Together*

In the last chapter I shared with you the story I realized my inbox was telling me—that in the midst of a time in my life where I lacked clarity, I was overdosing on a good thing. I was collecting gurus. I was seeking the right teachers at the wrong time.

While it's true we often need teachers and mentors to help us take our next right step, my tendency is to rush to other voices before I've taken the time to listen to my own voice as it is united with the voice of God. I've learned the importance of crafting a vision, or a bigger purpose, in solitude and silence first, then finding the teachers who can help me implement that vision with a plan.

If you have a big decision to make and you've taken the time to settle in and listen to the heartbeat of your own life, you may still feel unsettled with what comes next. Some of the best teachers available to us in our lives are ones we often overlook. I call them co-listeners, and they are infinitely more helpful than a gaggle of gurus. Here's how I found mine.

Earlier, I told you the story of what happened after John quit his job. I won't rehash the whole story here, since I've told it before, but I will summarize and say John and I were in the midst of a vocational transition and looking for answers. But we kept sensing God just leading us right back to each other. In the midst of a hard time, we wanted answers but all we got was arrows. And, as it turned out, those arrows led us home, just not in the way we thought. That was most of the story, but now I want to fill in one part I left out, because one of the arrows that led us on the journey pointed straight back to our own community.

Looking back on that time, it felt like a maze that looked normal except, when we worked it, the end was also the beginning. We came out the same way we went in. We worked it again, thinking we'd missed something along the way, but it kept bringing us back to where we started. In the midst of not knowing what was next (even more than the typical not-knowing what was next we all carry every day), we were following arrows through the grief of losing John's dad, arrows to one another, arrows to the heart of God, and finally arrows to our own local community.

When we weren't sure what do to next, we decided to intentionally gather a few people whom we loved in our house to listen to us say words and then see what they had to say back to us. We weren't asking for advice, exactly, although we were open to it. We knew better than to ask for answers, though we always hoped for them. Instead, we simply didn't want to feel so alone. We wanted people we loved and trusted to hear what we were saying, to see if there was something obvious we were missing, and to be with us in the midst of our uncertainty. And so, we made a list.

First, I wrote down the names of people and John wrote his own list separately. We did this because we didn't want to just ask our closest friends, although of course a few of them landed on our lists as well. Then we compared lists and saw we'd basically written down the same people. It was important to us to include people in different life stages than we were, people who had been around longer than we had and who had different perspectives than we did.

The night of our meeting, we sat in our living room, and I listened as John told this group of trusted friends about his grief, about his desire, and about his hope for the future. They listened. They understood. They saw us and heard us, asked us questions, and prayed for and with us. They also agreed to do it again with us a few months later.

As we continued to simply do the next right thing in our lives—pray together in the mornings, take the kids to school, write, read, go to the grocery store—eventually the arrow of community actually led to a vocational answer. It was from these few sessions with our co-listening group that John's next step became clear. At the time, that felt like the purpose. Over time, however, I've realized that part was secondary. Sometimes it looks like you're going nowhere, or that you're headed in the wrong direction. I'm learning that the decision itself is rarely the point. The point is becoming more fully ourselves in the presence of God, connecting with him and with each other, and living our lives as though we believe he is good and beautiful. The point is being honest about where you are and what you need, and then looking around in your own community for people to walk with you and with whom you can walk.

I spent years wishing people would support me only to later realize I was waiting around for something to come to me when I was perfectly capable of going out and getting it. I'm convinced God is less interested in where we end up than he is in who we are becoming. Whether we're employed or unemployed, encouraged or discouraged, filled with vision or fumbling in the fog, more than anything, our Father just wants to be with us. The most common way he shows his with-ness to us is in the actual, physical presence of other people.

○　○　○

The way we intentionally gathered people for the purpose of discernment might not be for everyone, but if you're in a season of transition or have a huge decision in front of you, and you feel stuck, hearing yourself say words in the company of some people you trust will be immensely valuable.

Gathering a group of people around you for the purpose of listening is not a new idea. A lot of us do this naturally in our families, with a group of friends, or with a small group or community group at our church. Some faith traditions do this as part of a regular practice.

At the time when John and I gathered a group we called "co-listeners," we had never heard of the Quaker practice of a Clearness Committee, but this discernment process they used, a method of listening designed to draw on the wisdom of other people, definitely shares some of the characteristics of what we had done. The job of those appointed to the Clearness Committee was to help a person discover whether there was clarity to move forward with a particular matter, whether they should wait, or if they should take other action. Quaker elder, author, and activist Parker Palmer describes this committee as the Quaker's answer to the question of how to deal with personal questions and problems. They didn't have clerical leaders, so they turned to one another.[1]

If you're in a time of transition and want to gather your own co-listening group, here are some simple things to keep in mind.

**One, do it on purpose.** It may be tempting not to make a big thing of it. Why not just talk to your friends or to your community group before or after your regular meeting time? Well, you can do both of those things. But there's something powerful about gathering people specifically for the purpose of listening, asking questions, and reflecting. At the very least, it will force you to do some deep thinking about the issue you're trying to discern in this transition because you'll want to be ready for the co-listeners' questions and insights. Ask people who don't just talk to hear themselves talk but who are thoughtful and good question-askers. In our case, our co-listening gathering was casual and conversational. Still, even though we didn't exactly know what we were doing, it was so helpful!

**Two, the co-listeners don't have to know one another, but they all need to know you well.** They need to be people you feel safe enough with so that you don't fear they will be judgey about your twisty, weird, insecure fears. There doesn't have to be very many of them—even two people sitting with you, listening to you, and being willing to ask you some questions could provide a lot of help and support for you. Be willing to look beyond your normal, everyday circles of people. You might be surprised who comes to mind.

**Finally, you have to ask them.** I know this seems obvious, but maybe you need the practical reminder. Reach out. State your need. Don't apologize. If they are unable to meet with you, let them say so. When you do meet, respect their time. Have a loose agenda, be as honest as you can, and try not to opinion-manage.

Keep the request short, to the point, and tell them you don't expect them to give you answers but simply would love to have their kind, listening presence to help you process this decision or transition. Tell them you are inviting a few people you can trust who will hear you and keep your confidence. You could also instruct the group to simply ask you questions rather than give you advice.

Now there's a chance you've been reading this entire chapter through narrowed eyes. Maybe this sounds either too hard or a little too good to be true. Remember, it doesn't have to be fancy. They don't have to be your best friends in the world. There doesn't have to be a gaggle of them. This is just one suggestion for you if you are staring a big decision in the face and you aren't sure where to turn.

I'm going to say something I can't fully prove, and maybe it goes against what we've heard all of our lives, but the longer I walk with our Father God, our friend Jesus, and the Holy Spirit who lives and dwells within us, the more I have a hunch that he isn't so concerned with the outcome of our decision, at least not in the same way we are. But he would be delighted to know that the decision we are carrying is moving us toward community and not away from it, that it is leading us to depend on others more and not less, and that it is turning our face toward his in a posture of listening with the hopeful expectation of receiving an answer.

If a hard decision can do all that? Then maybe we don't have to dread those decisions so much. Maybe we don't have to worry about what's going to happen next. Rather we can sit down on the inside and receive what's happening *now*, within us, beneath the rowdy surface, in the quiet center of our soul.

If you're standing at the crossroad of transition and you aren't sure which way to go, as you seek people in your life who can stand beside you, and as you are becoming a person who stands beside others, take heart—the Lord is always with you and within you, beside you and before you. He is not impatient, he is not angry, he is not overwhelmed by you. He is not frustrated, fed up, or afraid. He is filled with compassion toward you and his banner over you is love.

## ○ A PRAYER

*As we look for people to help us listen, remind us of what matters most.*

*The point is not a decision, a plan, or clarity.*

*The point is always union with you.*

*We want to remember that even in the midst of uncertainty, you remain faithful and true.*

*Help us to find people who will remind us of you and to be the kind of listener who does the same for others.*

## ○ A PRACTICE: **MAKE A LIST OF CO-LISTENERS**

Think about the people in your life who have some (or all) of these qualities, people who:

- ask thoughtful questions
- listen for the answers
- don't belittle you or say things that make you feel dumb
- don't take themselves too seriously
- take you just seriously enough

Finally, make a short list (maybe four to eight) of people you would consider asking to be part of a co-listening group. Consider people from your church, college friends, neighbors, family members, couples you admire, or longtime family friends. If you can't think of anyone, that's okay. Now you know what to look for.

*sixteen*

# CHOOSE YOUR ABSENCE

o o o

*The biggest deception of our digital age may be the lie that says we can be omni-competent, omni-informed, and omni-present.... We must choose our absence, our inability, and our ignorance—and choose wisely.*

Kevin DeYoung, *Crazy Busy*

Her table was cleared off exactly twice a year—Christmas Day and Easter Sunday. Every other day of the year, Grandma Morland's table was covered in stacks of newspaper, mail, bills, notepads, photographs, magazines, and those wonderfully thick Sears catalogs. If we needed to eat our cream-filled cookies or our popcorn covered in crazy-mixed-up salt, we would gently push a pile of papers toward the center of the table to make just enough space for our small paper towel.

If your soul has ever felt like Grandma Morland's kitchen table, I hope the process of reading this book is a way to practice clearing it off. Because one thing I know for sure is you need time and space—either to implement those things that matter or to finally figure out what they are.

One of the qualities I value most in a person is the ability to listen well. If I see you are a good listener, my respect for you immediately grows. If you don't look me in the eye or seem distracted, I may still like you but I probably won't trust you, and I definitely won't confide in you. I think that's probably true for most people. That's why one of the qualities I long to possess more of is *presence*.

Part of what it means to be a person of presence is to pay attention to what is happening around you—both in the place where you live and among the people who live there too. If you want to be a person of presence, it's important to pay attention to what is happening within you as well. But you can't be present to everything all the time. One way to cultivate presence might sound counterintuitive: it's actually by your absence. Not your absence from people or responsibility, but absence from the things that are keeping you from your people and your responsibilities. There's one thing in particular that may be causing you no small amount of stress and distraction. What is it?

It's called *opportunity*, and it starts like this. It could come in an email, through a conversation during a staff meeting, or via text, private message, personal invitation, or, heaven forbid, a phone call. However opportunities come, they present an invitation for you to do something you didn't plan on or expect. Maybe you're invited to take a trip, speak at a conference, participate in a group, apply for a particular job, serve on a board, write a column, teach a course, or volunteer in a classroom. I bet as I'm listing these things you already have something in mind.

Every new opportunity seems to have potential, at least at first. This may be especially true for certain personality types. We search the hopeful horizon for what this opportunity might bring us, define for us, or prove about us. Those invisible questions that hover beneath the surface raise their hands up high and seem to finally get some answers: *Do I have what it takes? Am I wanted? Do I belong?* For a moment, the invitation seems to shout a resounding *yes!* You have been asked, chosen, and invited. You are seen and valued. Come! Help! Teach! Lead! Volunteer!

If you are already unclear or unsure of your own calling, you may have a tendency to say yes as a default to these kinds of opportunities. Over time, these reactionary yeses can take their toll, and they could be the phantom cause of your current decision fatigue and lack of true presence in your own life.

It's true, some great opportunities are exactly that—great. Fantastic, even. I am not actually here to tell you to choose your absence from great opportunities. But just because some-one presents an idea as a great one does not make it so. Every opportunity is not created equal, and you get to decide along with God whether something is great for you or not.

When an opportunity presents itself, take a little time to consider where this opportunity will actually lead and call it that, with words. Things often seem great when we leave them in ambiguity. But when we get down to the details we start to see the truth of things. Here are some questions you can ask yourself when opportunities come your way. There is not a right or wrong answer, and some will be more relevant depending on your situation:

Will you get paid for this?

Are the expectations clear?

Would you actually enjoy it?

Is it something you've always wanted to do?

Does it involve a meaningful partnership?

If you were in a room of people and this was called out into the crowd, would you raise your hand to volunteer for it?

If this great opportunity is something you're not getting paid for, will take an amount of time that can't be measured, cannot be clearly defined, or is something you don't really want to do, then this opportunity could be one you need to choose your absence from. This is not easy, because the phrase that continues to haunt you is this one: "But it's such a great opportunity."

When we say that, what we often mean is other people would jump at the chance, and who am I to turn this down when they would love to do it? But just because someone else would want it is not a good reason for you to say yes. I know that sounds like middle-school advice, but when I actually look at my own life, it is something that gives me pause. So here's a little practice for you to try, to test if this potential next thing is actually your next *right* thing.

Say you've received an invitation from a colleague you admire to participate in something prestigious (use your imagination as to how that applies to your own life). The decision to do it or not lands squarely in your lap. It is what many in your circles would call a great opportunity.

Do you have the opportunity in mind? Good. Now finish this sentence: "I want to say yes to this because it would be a great opportunity to _____."

The phrase "It's a great opportunity" is not actually a complete sentence, at least not here.

A great opportunity to ... *what*? The literal definition of *opportunity* is "a set of circumstances that makes it possible to do something." If it's true that this thing is actually a great opportunity for you, you have to be able to finish the sentence.

For example, you may finish your sentence in one of these ways: "I want to do this thing because it would be a great opportunity to ...

See the world
Love my neighbor
Learn a new skill
Meet new people
Be with my kids
Walk with God

Make one million dollars

Serve my family

Have fun

Grow my business

These and countless more could all be valid reasons for a person to do a thing.

Finishing this sentence is a start, but it's not complete. For example, let's say you do this little exercise and you finish the sentence like this: "This invitation would be a great opportunity to grow my business."

The next question you need to ask yourself is, Is this a season of my life where I am working on growing my business? Is that part of what I've already decided is a high priority right now? This may be a good thing, even a right thing, but is it *my next right thing*?

If yes—then go for it! This sounds like it could be great for you. But remember, just because the person who issues the invitation says it's a great opportunity, and just because it might lead to something you might want to have happen, doesn't make it an automatic yes for you. When opportunities come your way, you have the opportunity (ha!) to discern between your values and your vanity.

Oftentimes I think something *could be* a great opportunity, so I say yes out of a fear of missing out. I may also say yes because I want everyone to know I was invited. Looking back, though, it's maybe about one in ten opportunities that turn out to be great. That's not exact math, but when I consider my own inbox and my own conversations, that seems to be about right. The other nine "opportunities" turn out to be one of three things: a job, an obligation, or a glorified favor. We call these things opportunities because we think maybe they'll get us something we want, but oftentimes, if we really look hard at them, it's a myth.

Again, I'm not saying you should never say yes to those things. We do jobs, we have obligations, and we offer people favors all the time. But call them what they are: a job, an obligation, or a favor. Don't call them great opportunities.

○   ○   ○

Bonita Lillie is a woman who mentored me for many years in my writing, both from a distance and in person. As you consider the opportunities that may come your way, consider these words Bonita sent to me years ago in an email as I was working to discern my next right thing. She shared with me a bit of her own story, and her words still resonate with me today.

> In the stillness, when all other voices were silent, I heard *His* voice speaking to me. And He was leading and guiding and clarifying and redefining. The vision becomes clear. And with that clarity, I was empowered to make decisions. Instead of yielding to or even entertaining every request put before me, I am able to say, "I do this. I only do this. I don't do that." You are the sole carrier of the vision God has given you. No one else has it. You are the visionary. Trust the vision.

This is a practice in discernment, and it isn't easy. As you begin to filter requests through this lens, you'll also begin to know when to choose your absence on purpose from these mythical great opportunities so that you can be present to what matters most. Let's get quiet and listen to the heartbeat of our own lives rather than looking outside of ourselves for better, more important opportunities. Choose your absence so that your presence will have more impact.

This will not be easy, especially if your fear of missing out is particularly strong. But if you remember Christ dwells within you, beside you, behind you, and before you, he will remind you of what really matters. Ask him, then listen well. Your work is your work. Your pace is your pace. Your life is your life. What a gift.

○ A PRAYER

*We confess how our hunger for power can disguise itself in surprisingly creative ways, like the promise of a great opportunity.*

*Forgive us for how often we choose our vanity over our values. Be our wisdom as we discern the difference.*

*Protect us from the mythology of opportunity and the fear of missing out.*

○ A PRACTICE: **TAKE ANOTHER LOOK AT AN OPPORTUNITY**

Living attentive and paying attention is one of my favorite ways to live, but I've discovered if I do it in the wrong order, by going outward before I move inward, then I may add to the stress and distraction in my life in ways I never intended. Pick an invitation you're considering right now and finish this sentence: "This will be a great opportunity to _____." Then be honest: Is this the season for you to actually engage in that great opportunity?

## *seventeen*

# FIND A NO MENTOR

○  ○  ○

*If the person you are trying so hard not to disappoint will be displeased by a no, they'll eventually be disappointed even if you say yes.*

Lysa TerKeurst, *The Best Yes*

Sometimes, in order to remain true to your life, to your people, and to your own calling, you need to turn down what others may call great opportunities and choose your absence from them. You may walk through the exercise in the previous chapter and determine that your current great opportunity is actually just a big ol' favor you aren't able to commit to right now. It's one thing to know that; it's another thing to actually say no.

My sister, Myquillyn, is someone I turn to when I have trouble saying no.[1] If you know you need to say no but you lack courage to do it, you could benefit from a No Mentor. It's a title Myquillyn came up with years ago that started off as sort of a joke because she was always telling me not to do stuff. Over time, as I would take her advice, I realized saying no became easier for me. Again, I don't do so for the sake of just saying no but because the good things I turn down make way for the great things I am called to. As I've realized how valuable her direction has become for me, this No Mentorship thing has become a vital part of my decision-making life. I know when I have a tough decision to make, especially when I'm leaning on no but don't have the confidence to throw all my weight into it, she will be there to remind me what I value, what I'm about, what I have time for, and what I truly want to do.

The No Mentor is a special kind of person. While a regular mentor will help you weigh decisions and give valuable advice, a No Mentor goes in with a stronger filter from the beginning. Most likely, this person will help you choose your absence from the things you already know should be a no but it's hard for you to admit. Unlike your co-listening group members, who have a primary role of listening, your No Mentor will be no-nonsense, straightforward, and unapologetic. She will not be deterred by glitz or glamor. She is not fooled by shiny objects or mirrored balls. She is relentlessly on your side and has the health of your soul, your family, and your work in mind. Sometimes, this person will convince you to say yes—but this is rare and not the norm.

If you don't have a No Mentor in your life, one friend or sister or brother who will help you eliminate the unessential, then maybe finding one is your next right thing. Here's what you're looking for.

**First, you need someone who makes decisions the way you want to make them in the areas you want to make them in.** In the same way you wouldn't take fashion advice from someone who dresses in a way you don't like, don't take scheduling advice from someone whose schedule makes you want to hide under your coffee table. When you're trying to make a decision about your schedule, for example, asking the preschool parent who is always late, flustered, and distracted is a terrible idea. Likewise, asking the go-getter with a high capacity for people and activity might also not be best if you don't share this person's energy level. This might seem obvious, but we tend to ask the most easily accessible people for advice rather than considering if the people around us are actually modeling the life we want to live.

**Second, you need someone who knows you *and* gets the subtleties of your decision in a way other people might not.** For example, I'm an author, and sometimes I'm invited to be part of cool things in that capacity, so it helps to either ask a fellow author or at least someone who semi-gets the work I do to be a No Mentor for me in that area rather than someone who would tell me to do it just because it would be a cool thing. I'm lucky that my sister is also an author, so she sees through the mythology of opportunity and knows when something could be great for me or when it just *sounds* great. It's important to note here that a No Mentor is someone who knows *you* and gets the subtleties of *your* decision. My sister has often advised me to say yes to things that she would never say yes to. But that's because our gifting and our goals are different. A good No Mentor knows how to differentiate between her stuff and your stuff.

**Third, you need someone you can trust with the underbelly.** Every choice has an underbelly—whether that is a season of life, a particular phobia you have, or a recurring argument you and your spouse always have about a particular issue. Your No Mentor has to know the whole story, the ugly and weird and twisty, which means you have to be able to trust her. If she doesn't know the whole story, she might say, "Yes, take that opportunity to travel to Hawaii to network with those cool people!" without realizing how travel makes you seven shades of nervous, how those cool people are conniving and cutthroat and include your ex-boyfriend, and how you are allergic to the sun. Tell it all and tell it true. Your No Mentor can handle it.

**Finally, you need someone who respects you but isn't *impressed* by you.** This one is tricky and is why my sister was the perfect pick for me. She respects me and loves me and has my best interest in mind. But she isn't impressed by me in the sense that I can do no wrong or I'm so cool. It's hard to fool a girl who knows you as her dorky baby sister who played Barbies way past an acceptable age.

There's a chance you already have a No Mentor in your life. Maybe your next right thing is just to make it official. That doesn't mean you have to ask her to be your No Mentor. She may not even know you call her that. Build a conversation with her into your normal decision-making process when you get stuck or have something you are leaning on no for but need help going all the way. Make it a natural next right step to ask her if she would be willing to help you process a decision you have to make.

A No Mentor is not there to keep you from doing things you want to do. And finding one is not an excuse to say no to stuff you *don't* want to do. We are kingdom people and, in a real way, our time doesn't belong to us; it all belongs to God. The problem is we've misunderstood what that means. Instead of being people who look within and discern where he is leading us, we look around and overcommit ourselves. When the whispers of our calling try to speak to us, we don't have the time or the space to listen.

A No Mentor is there to help you feel confident about saying no to the things you really don't want to do anyway or to help you finally discover your strong, brave yes in the midst of fear. We all need a friend we can trust who is willing to go deep with us, to listen, to offer feedback, and to help us either solve a problem or feel better about the fact that the problem is unsolvable.

What inevitably will happen the more you run things by your No Mentor is this: eventually, you'll learn to be your own.

Maybe you're picking up on a pattern here, but a big part of discerning your next right step is knowing and understanding what you really want to do. Knowing what you want isn't selfish; it's actually crucial to making decisions because it builds confidence, hastens healing, and is a gift to the people you love. The simplest benefit to knowing what you really want? It helps you choose your absence by saying yes and no to things without all the angst.

I mentioned Bonita, my writing mentor, in the last chapter. She taught me early on about how only I carry the vision for my writing (business, parenting, career, and ministry). No one else does. Just because you're good at something doesn't mean you're supposed to start a business doing that thing, write a book about it, lead a team through it, teach it, get a degree in it, or anything at all. Even if everyone tries to tell you that you should. Even if you could make a lot of money for it. Even if it makes a lot of sense. Even if people tell you you're crazy not to. Only you carry the vision. The better you know and communicate that, the more content and effective you will be. Wisdom from others can be a wonderful thing, but just know when you seek counsel from him and them and her it can also breed chaos and confusion. Pick your mentors wisely.

And if no one comes to mind right now? That's okay. Maybe your next right thing is to be your own No Mentor and to pray for a person to come into your life who could walk alongside you in this way. Refuse to feel bad here for what you don't yet have. In fact, the best way to ensure that more No Mentors are out there is to be a No Mentor for somebody else.

When a friend comes to you with a question, a problem, or a tough decision, take a step back. Ask lots of questions and listen to her answers. Listen to both what she says and what she fails to say. Watch how her body rises or falls when she talks. Listen to her tone and her excuses. See if her eyes light up when she talks about the thing. Will she look you in the eye? Does she use the word "should" a lot? Does she sound motivated by guilt, shame, or pressure? Consider the under-belly. Be on the side of her soul. Stand up for her in ways she may not yet have the courage to stand up for herself.

## ○ A PRAYER

*Our time is in your hands.*

*We confess all the ways we have tried to manage it rather than surrender it to you.*

*May we continue to cultivate a strong no in our lives so that we can say more life-giving yeses.*

*Be gentle with us as we have for so long insisted we can do life on our own.*

*Show us the mentors who will remind us who we are and help us to discern our next right thing in love.*

## ○ A PRACTICE: REFLECT ON YES AND NO

Always remember that, in the kingdom of God, all things are being made new, including our poorly chosen yeses. Even so, past decisions can help inform future ones.

Reflect on a time in your life when you said yes to something only to realize later it was perhaps not a wise yes. What was the situation surrounding that yes? Did anyone encourage or discourage you in that decision? What was the outcome?

Now think of a time when you said a brave no to what many might consider a great opportunity. What was the situation surrounding that no? Did anyone encourage or discourage you in that decision? What was the outcome?

## *eighteen*
# DON'T GIVE YOUR CRITIC WORDS

o   o   o

*If this horse is dead, it's time to dismount.*

Christine Caine

We stand on the corner of Randolph and Green after a breakfast of sourdough toast, housemade sausage, blueberry pancakes, and coffee with raw sugar. The Uber pulls up and we climb inside, falling into easy conversation with the driver.

"You know that chef Vivian Howard?" she asks, after learning I live in North Carolina, where Vivian is from.

I tell her no, but I met her at a book signing once. "Oh, yeah, she did write a book," she says.

Turns out, our driver is also a chef, but for now she's feeling burned out. Driving meets the need she has for conversation, and she takes the long way through the city to prove it. As she and my friend Shannan make small talk in the front seat, I pull up the driver's profile in my Uber app. To be quite honest, I'm wondering if her oh-so-friendly decision to take the long way to show us the sights is going to run up the meter. Do Ubers work like cabs? I can't remember, so I try to find out. While I'm in the app, I notice her reviews.

"You have great reviews!" I say it from the backseat, careful not to stare at my screen too long, my attempt to keep the backseat dizziness from catching up with me.

"Yeah, they're pretty good," she says. She tells us a few colorful stories about driving an Uber, the kinds of people she's met, the stories that we wouldn't believe they tell her. She seems to like her job, the questions we ask and the captive audience we give her.

"It's a good job," she says, "and I've never had a problem." She pauses now, and then she says this: "Except that one lady that one time." My ears perk up, ready for a story. She's already told us so many stories in our short commute; this one is sure to shape up as the best one yet.

The story doesn't come. Instead, she says this about that one lady that one time: "But we're not gonna give her words, 'cause that's exactly what she wants."

Shannan turns around and looks at me; our eyes meet big and impressed.

"We're not gonna give her words." I repeat it instinctively, trying out the phrase on my lips, catching her wisdom, repeating it slow, a responsive reading in a backseat church.

Later, Shannan and I will have a conversation about that phrase, unsure of how it went, exactly. I meant to write it down in the moment, but I got distracted by the driver's next story. She went in for an eye appointment and came out with a diagnosis for a brain tumor, and I'm still trying to decide if I believe her.

In the end, we'll agree this phrase captures the truth of what that Uber driver said about her critic in the car that one hot day in Chicago: *we're not gonna give her words.*

The critic only lives if we let her live. And I don't mean the critic that is helpful and has your best interest at heart. This isn't someone in your co-listening group or one of your No Mentors. I mean the spiteful one, the petty one, the one who said those things way back when. Maybe the one who lives in your own head. That time is past, and the only voice that critic could have now in your life? It's yours.

How would today be different or how would your next decision change if you refused to give the critic words?

Shannan smiles as the car turns right onto Navy Pier, and says, "This is gonna be your next podcast episode, isn't it?" This girl knows me well.

○   ○   ○

The critic is a tricky companion, because not all critics are created equal. Just because someone is critical doesn't automatically mean you should ignore them and call them a hater. But it also doesn't automatically mean they're right. We can learn a lot from critique, from correction, from critical thinking and direction. But the trouble comes when we allow all critical voices to weigh the same amount.

When it comes to making decisions, combating decision fatigue, and learning to trust our own heart in the presence of God, we have to be careful who we allow in. Here's something I've learned about the critics in our lives: it's not necessary (or healthy, for that matter) to have people always agree with you, but the critiques to most seriously consider are the ones coming from those who *believe* in you. If someone who believes in you, your work, your art, or your decisions is pointing out a weakness or trying to make things better, it's helpful and healthy to consider their words with humility and grace. Resist the urge to close yourself off from them. Instead, open yourself in the presence of Christ and allow his words to partner with their critique in order to show you the truth. This is the critic who gets to have words.

But if the critic not only disagrees with you but also doesn't believe in you, their words may be more difficult to sort out. Like that stranger on the internet. The offhand opinion your brother's girlfriend's sister's roommate has of your Instagram feed. The angry customer who, no matter how graciously you apologize or how much you try to make it right, just refuses to be satisfied. These are the ones who have the least right to influence your life but somehow, for some reason, end up getting the most power.

How do I know? Because right now, I feel sure you can remember a particular critical voice in your mind, and you remember their words exactly. So, what's your next right thing in this moment? It's time to call a truce.

We aren't going to change their minds. Instead, let's change ours. Let's stop giving that critic words. Let's stop handing her the mic. Let's take her seat away from the table and put it out in the hall. Our friend Jesus knows what it means to be questioned, challenged, humiliated, and critiqued. Not once ever did he allow a negative critic to change one solitary decision he made on earth. He was about his Father's business, and all was well with him. His face was set like a flint. His soul was always at peace. His countenance remained kind. His choice was always love.

Here is the thing it all comes down to, the thing it always comes down to in the kingdom of God, where our belief slams right into our everyday life. The critic points out my weakness and my fear, but if I'm paying attention, he will also point out something else, a gift I would never dare to ask for and a motivation he never means to give. The gift the critic brings, whether we like it or not, is a line in the sand. When the critic says words, we have to decide if we believe them. We have to decide who gets to have a say.

The voice of the critic forces us to face our biggest fears and, in turn, listen hard for the voice of God. I can worry or I can work. I can get stuck or I can move on. I can get defensive or I can be free. Instead of giving the critic words, here are some new words to consider:

I believe in the power of life.

I believe in the holy resurrection.

I believe nothing can separate me from the love of God.

I believe I am set free.

## ○ A PRAYER

*As we consider the decisions that weigh heavy on our minds, we don't want to give our critic words.*

*Keep us in our stillness.*

*Quiet us in your presence.*

*Remind us of your love.*

*Replace the words of the critic with your words of peace.*

*As we lean our ear toward your heartbeat, allow our voices to rise up in your presence.*

*Then be our courage as we simply do our next right thing in love.*

## ○ A PRACTICE: CATCH YOURSELF IN THE ACT

When it comes to making decisions, combating decision fatigue, and learning to trust our own heart in the presence of God, we have to be careful who we allow in. This is difficult, though, because for most of us (all of us?) the critical voice in our head is so familiar, we barely realize its power.

Today, pay attention to ways you may be giving your critic words, whether your critic is real or imagined. Ask Jesus to help you catch yourself in the act of repeating that negative opinion, texting your cousin words your coworker said about you, or rehearsing your defensive response in the shower. Pay attention to your posture when you repeat these negative, often hurtful phrases. Remember in Christ you have everything you need. Don't give your critic words today.

*nineteen*

# COME HOME TO YOURSELF

○　○　○

*It's a wild and wonderful thing to bump
into someone and realize it's you.*

Fil Anderson

hope your jagged edges are beginning to smooth, allowing you to feel the presence of Jesus with you in every ordinary moment. I hope these words are creating space for your soul to breathe so that you can name the unnamed things within you and discern your next right thing in love. I hope your narrative of God is shaping into one that is more true than false, and that, through his Spirit, you're beginning to loosen your grip on outcomes. This simple, soulful decision-making path isn't linear, is it? It starts out that way, maybe, but then it dips down into a cool, shadowed valley and meanders into the dark of the woods. Just when you're sure you're lost, the trees open up into a wide field, a green pasture near still water. And then we start again.

We've looked at the various people we turn to, for better or worse, when we struggle with decisions. We've become honest about our guru collection and made a list of potential co-listeners. We're aware of our need for a No Mentor in our life and we've decided not to give our critic words, always with the assurance of God's presence working in, through, and around us. But there's another person walking with you on this path who may not be as obvious to you.

Too often the relational interaction we engage in the most is also the one that is most often ignored. It's the relationship we have with ourselves. So, here we are again, discerning our next steps and our right-nows in the midst of *Now what?* and *Why did this happen? Again?* When life becomes unpredictable and unsure, it's easy to scatter apart in panic, to come undone, to be spread too thin, to forget who and where we are.

This is good for exactly no one. God always wants us to know it's not too late to come on back—to be gathered back to center again. What if your next right thing is to settle in right where you are and come back home to yourself? Sound strange? Consider this: the only person you're guaranteed to be with every day of your life is you. It doesn't get much more *home* than that. So maybe it's time to make some peace.

○   ○   ○

We lived in a white house with a gravel drive on Gladstone Avenue in Columbus, Indiana, until I was in the fourth grade. Sisters Missy and Shelly lived with their mom on one side of us, and I thought they were rich or lucky because they had a basement, a sandbox, *and* cable TV. On the other side of our house lived red-headed Michelle, who never outgrew her baby teeth and always smelled like ketchup. A couple doors down from her was a tiny house set back from the street where Mr. Huntington lived.

He was a skeleton of a man, eyes shadowed by protruding eyebrows, all angles, no curves, a praying mantis with no faith at all. Through elementary school, our bus stop was at the end of Mr. Huntington's driveway, delivering a low-grade anxiety into the pit of my stomach every school morning. I vaguely remember his front windows, covered with orange-and-black No Trespassing signs, makeshift glasses on a haunted house that never stopped watching us. I can't say for sure, but standing on his driveway definitely felt like a violation of those threatening signs.

My shoulders stayed tense until bus 25 came around the corner to pick us up for school; it was always a relief to step off the forbidden property and into the warm, loud interior of our school bus. From the safety of my green pleather bus seat, I found the courage to glance back at the house. It was hard enough standing at the edge of his driveway. I can't even imagine walking up to his door.

And yet, in many ways, I've had a lot of experience in walking up to the door of a house where I feel unwanted and unwelcome, because for years this is what I did to myself. I stood at the edge of the driveway of my own soul, unaware of the life that wanted to be lived on the other side of the door.

Coming home to yourself is not always an easy thing to do.

If you arrive at a house and the hostess stands on the porch shouting criticisms, judgments, and sarcasms at you, guess what you won't want to do? Walk through the door. You will turn your back on that house every time and vow never to return. What if we stopped standing on our own front porch and bullying ourselves? What if we decided, instead, to be a gracious hostess to ourselves at the threshold of our own soul?

We don't go home when home is unsafe. Maybe your next right thing today is to recognize all the ways you've become your own enemy, all the ways you've put No Trespassing signs on your own soul windows, all the ways you've become your own suspicious, furrow-browed neighbor.

What does it mean to come home to ourselves, and how can this help us make decisions? God is always giving us hints about who we are and how he has made us to image himself in the world. He doesn't shout, though, which is why becoming a soul minimalist is so important. Because it clears out the clutter that comes at us in our daily lives and helps us pay attention. One way God often invites us to see ourselves is through the words of other people.

Instead of dismissing people's words when they sincerely offer a kind word about you, or gratitude for something you've done or the person you are, practice listening instead and see if their words might carry a hint to your design. In the summer of 2016, I sat with a group of writers tucked into a hillside in Tuscany, and as the evening crept into night, my friend Tsh said she appreciated my friendship, and when we related, she felt pastored by me. Pastored. She used that word. When she said it, something caught within me, a light both foreign and familiar, and the tears stung and the light grew and I knew she spoke something true. I'm still growing into that shepherding role and I have a lot to learn, but when she spoke those words that night she colored something in for me, and it was well with my soul.

Think back to words someone spoke to you that, when they said them, made you feel fully seen and fully known to the extent that you could say along with them, "There I am." This isn't simply positive affirmation. Just because someone said something positive doesn't mean it felt like *you*. If you were told when you were younger how responsible and dependable you were, that's a really positive thing and may have been nice for you to hear, but it could have also felt more like an expectation to live up to rather than a truth for you to grow into.

In contrast, I had an English teacher in high school, Mrs. Smith, tell me I was a good writer. When she said it, it didn't feel like something I had to try to prove; it just felt true, even though it would take decades before I grew into it. On the other hand, I also had a teacher who, when I finished up college, told me I should get my master's degree in Deaf education because she knew I would be good at it, and though I was flattered, and she may have even been right, it just didn't ring true. It just didn't feel quite like home to me.

I wonder if you can think of a time when you felt most like yourself. Where were you? What were you doing? Who were you with? And maybe it's also important to consider, Who were you *not* with? These questions can help you begin to get familiar with your own giftedness, personality, and offerings you're made to give. As my friend and teacher Fil Anderson says, "It's a wild and wonderful thing to bump into someone and realize it's you." What does it mean for you to come home to yourself? It will be different for all of us, and it may even come as you try something new. I can't say specifically what this might look like for you, but I can say when you're close, you'll know it. It will sound soft and gentle. It will feel safe and settled. You won't feel like you have something to prove. It will be kind and open and free. It may be something that you'll feel invited to grow into, that will require a bit of a journey. But it's one you'll be glad to take.

## ○ A PRAYER

*O God, help me to believe the truth about myself no matter how beautiful it is.*

Macrina Weidekehr[1]

## ○ A PRACTICE: **REMEMBER WHO YOU ARE**

Think of a time when you felt most like yourself. Now think of words others have said that have affirmed this in your life.

If you have trouble coming up with some of those words, you have a God who always fills in the gaps. In his presence is where you will find yourself. And in the presence of your true self is where you will finally see God.

As you consider what it means for you to make peace on the inside, here are some final, familiar words from Psalm 139:

> O LORD, You have searched me and known me.
> You know when I sit down and when I rise up;
> You understand my thought from afar.
> You scrutinize my path and my lying down,
> And are intimately acquainted with all my ways.
> (vv. 1–3)

*This is the Word of the Lord. Thanks be to God.*

*twenty*

# PICK WHAT YOU LIKE

o o o

*If God gives such attention to the appearance of wildflowers—most of which are never even seen—don't you think he'll attend to you, take pride in you, do his best for you?*

Matthew 6:30 *Message*

It's Saturday and I'm standing in the middle of the garden center, frozen. I have one plant in my cart, a tiny bright-green ivy that caught my eye. Beyond that, I'm stuck and beginning to feel that familiar discouragement I get when confronted with a simple decision that has many options in an area where I don't have a lot of confidence.

A week ago, I walked with John through the bright, warm streets of the coastal city of Coronado, situated across the San Diego Bay from downtown San Diego. It was our last day in California and we spent it browsing the shops and taking our time, enjoying the company and the scenery. From the rocky coastline to the constant cool breeze, California doesn't mess around. It's beautiful; I would even call it enchanting in some ways, and I found myself paying attention to both the grand things and the small things that made an impression.

We come from the exact opposite coast, the southeastern part of the United States, with thick air, tall trees, lush green leaves, gentle hills, and grass in every yard. Here in Southern California, it became a game to try to find a yard with grass. Mostly we saw geometric rock gardens covered in thick, hardy plants with waxy leaves and vibrant, bold flowers.

Dear California, what you lack in grass, you make up for in succulents. In front of nearly every store was a pot or container with a collection of succulents: Irish Mint, Little Jewel, Painted Lady. Succulents have the best names.

Walking those streets, I decided I wanted more plants in my life. I could picture in my mind what I wanted, could imagine going and picking things out and filling our house and porch and yard with green in every shade. I was happy about it, looking forward to it, and glad to get started.

That brings us back to me, standing in the garden center, frozen.

The discouragement barrels down fast. It's familiar, annoying, and kind of ridiculous. Because it's one thing to feel overwhelmed in a situation that matters, like a new job, a new role, a new marriage, a new school, or a new business endeavor. But it feels dumb to let discouragement seep in for something as small as picking out plants. Still, that's where I find myself: with a big idea, a lot of options, and an almost-empty shopping cart.

Granted, this moment of indecision is small-scale and inconsequential in the scheme of life. Still, these moments come for all of us. If it doesn't hit you in the garden center, it will come in the grocery store or standing in your kitchen trying to cook. Maybe it's related to which book to read next or how to wrap a gift in a pretty way, without it looking like a toddler did it, or choosing a paint color for a room. Though the situations differ, they have one thing in common: they are all supposed to be fun, delightful parts of life. But instead, for some reason and for some of us, they take a turn into feelings of being overwhelmed, discouraged, and personally shamed. What we hope will be life-giving turns out to be life-draining, one more decision we feel incapable of making.

This isn't the first time I've stood in the garden center with high hopes, only to feel incapable and overcome once I get there. What does it look like to just start or to start over, to take a next right step toward something we want even if we feel unsure?

You could start by acknowledging the fear. I can't tell you the number of times I've swept an emotion aside because it didn't feel valid. *Overwhelmed at the garden center? What a luxury! There are people with real problems in the world!* Well, that's true. What is also true is we can't move through what we refuse to acknowledge. And usually, the small things are simply arrows pointing to some bigger things. Shame in the garden center is evidence of shame in other areas as well. If my knee-jerk reaction to a simple decision like picking out plants is shame and feeling overcome, then can you imagine what my knee-jerk reaction must be in areas of life that really matter and have consequence?

If you feel besieged by the small, inconsequential decisions of daily life, take a moment to acknowledge this feeling of smallness. Admit that this decision shouldn't be a big deal but for some reason it is. For now, this is what we know. Fear, we see you. We acknowledge you. But you don't get the final say.

Once you've named the feeling, accept that you are allowed to be here.

Having pretty flowers, painting a room a bold color, or trying out a new recipe is not reserved for people who know more, who have more, or who seem to be more than you. This is for you too. You don't have to be fancy, rich, chosen, or special. You just get to be you. You are allowed to take up space in the room. You are allowed to choose something and you are allowed to change your mind.

While I am standing here looking at plants, a phrase arrives in my mind complete, like a green leaf falling onto the grass in summer. *Pick what you like, then see how it grows.* In my head, it sounds like my own voice, but it doesn't feel like my idea.

Relieved, I push the cart through the leafy aisles, wheels thumping over a garden hose, barely visible mist appearing on my arms. I wonder when plant growing and picking got so complicated in my mind. But it did, and admitting it was half the battle. After that, it's just time to pick.

Pick what you like, then see how it grows.

I've assumed it's normal to have to learn some things in life, like how to read, write, and use a computer. But for some reason, I think taking care of plants should come naturally. It's not like that, though. This is also something that could be and, if you want to, should be learned. But we have to start somewhere, and the beginning is as good a place as any. So pick what you like, then see how it grows.

I put some plants in my cart. I grab one with a tag that says, "I like low light," and I think of a place it could go. I pick another with the name "jenny" in it, because that feels friendly. *Pick what you like, then see how it grows.*

As I continue to carry that phrase with me, I think of all the ways it can be true, in lots of situations. Did your boss ask you to choose the location for the staff retreat? Trying to decide on a major in college next year? Have a day to yourself coming up and don't want to waste it but do want to know how to spend it well? Pick what you like, then see how it grows. Just this, in as many situations as possible.

I know this little story is only a small example of all the ways you may be starting over, starting again, or starting out for the first time. No matter the size or scope, new beginnings always come with a mix of all kinds of emotions. I realize we bear the weight of decisions uniquely. What causes some to be overwhelmed may be delightful for others. Perhaps you can't relate to this kind of hesitancy I felt in the garden center because you always know what you want, or at least you're willing to take small risks in things that don't matter so much, like picking out plants. We could learn a lot from you. Because those of us who struggle with choices spend a lot of time not only going around and around the choices in our minds but also kicking ourselves for making the thing so hard in the first place. If that's you, you're in good company. Pick what you like, then see how it grows. If that little plant dies in a week, well, then you've learned something. But another outcome is also possible. *What if it blooms?*

○ **A PRAYER**

*As we stand at new beginnings and grieve those long goodbyes, teach us what it means to hold on to what we need for the journey and gently let the rest go.*

*Father, you bring new mercies every morning and give us the grace to start over as many times as we might need.*

*Keep pace with us as we learn to keep pace with you.*

*Thank you for not rolling your eyes when we find ourselves here again.*

*Give us the courage to pick what we like and the patience to see how it grows.*

○ **A PRACTICE: PICK WHAT YOU LIKE**

For some, this might be the hardest practice in the whole book. At first glance it seems harmless, even obvious. But when we attempt to practice it, we hesitate. Could it be possible this is a partial root of a lot of our decision fatigue? Could it be possible that this freedom is one we've never been able to indulge? For today, when you stand in the garden, the classroom, the office, the paint store, the library, the sanctuary, or the street, accept that there may not be a perfect choice, a right choice, or an ideal. Instead, pick what you like, then see how it grows.

*twenty-one*

# WEAR BETTER PANTS

o  o  o

*One of the ways we punish ourselves for not being more or better or thinner or stronger is by trying to squeeze ourselves—force ourselves, even—into all kinds of ill-fitting relationships. With other people, with ourselves, with our pants.*

Leeana Tankersley, *Breathing Room*

Wearing better pants has become my favorite spiritual discipline.

As you continue to pay attention to ways you can come home to yourself, it's helpful to find spiritual disciplines, or practices, that support this endeavor—and even better when they're weird and quirky and personal to you. In the midst of a busy schedule, a load of laundry, a painful diagnosis, a confusing conversation, or prep for that upcoming trip, it's easy to forget your center. It's easy to forget who you are. Some of our self remains hidden beneath piles of daily activity we can see and shadows of shame we often can't see. Perhaps today, your next right thing is to release something you no longer need so that you can move one step closer to becoming who you already are.

When I graduated from high school, my youth pastor gave all us seniors a book on the spiritual disciplines. Good girl that I was, I marked that book up in all the best ways, determined to tackle a discipline a week for however long it took to become the best possible version of myself: prayer, Scripture reading, fasting, whatever. I knew I couldn't be perfect, but I thought it would be all right to get closer than anyone else.

Several years of Bible college, marriage, and mothering later, I realized that the good girl in my head was a perfectly annoying mirage, and if I wanted to really know Jesus and be a sane person, I had to let go of my constant attempts at trying to earn acceptance and the ridiculous idea that I could perform my way into being loved.[1]

One of the casualties of my good girl detox was shedding my misconceptions about discipline and spiritual practices. It might sound extreme, but sometimes it's necessary. I needed to give myself permission not to practice some things for a while because I couldn't figure out how to do them without thinking I was earning something. The past eight years or so have been a reentry of sorts into the world of the spiritual disciplines for me. It's different now: kinder, gentler, tender, and more free. My definitions have changed, as has (I hope) my demeanor.

I now understand the fundamental truth beneath the spiritual disciplines, that, as author and philosopher Dallas Willard says, "If a discipline is not producing freedom in me, it's probably the wrong thing for me to be doing."[2]

Practicing a spiritual discipline is not about trying to earn something, prove something, or win. Practicing a spiritual discipline is more about receiving power to live in the kingdom. It's about being aware of the presence of God and putting myself there on purpose so that my character might be transformed. It's about training my mind and my will to practice what my heart deeply believes. It's about knowing that each moment is packed with grace, but sometimes I need practice to see it. It's about becoming the person I already am in Christ. Anything can be a spiritual discipline when we recognize the presence of God with us in it. It could be something we do, but I'm also learning a discipline can also be something we undo.

o   o   o

I confess I have had to unlearn some things I've always believed about spirituality and the spiritual disciplines. Aside from the false belief that I thought I needed to work for my own acceptance, I've also made spirituality too small. I've put it in a box labeled "invisible things," which may in some ways be true but is also, in many ways, untrue. This came to the surface for me in a most unexpected way, on the floor of my bedroom as I cleaned out my closet.

During a week when I had some major deadlines to meet, I did exactly what any respectable writer would do. I set my face like a flint in the direction of the messiest corners of my house and decided now was the perfect time to engage in a good purge. My closets are never more organized than when I have a writing deadline. I started in my bedroom and began to sift through clothes. At the bottom of one of my drawers, I found some loved but long-forgotten jeans, pulled them on, and continued to tidy up around the house, moving from room to room without a plan but with an eye for tidying, straightening, and getting rid of trash and clutter and the things that pile up.

As I moved through the house with a trash bag, tackling the piles and purging clutter, I noticed a shift, ever so slight. My energy and my motivation began to sag. Usually decluttering and straightening give me new energy, so I paused for a moment to consider why my shoulders were drooping, why my eyebrows were furrowed, and why I felt so fussy. When I retraced my steps, I found it. It was the jeans, the favorite ones I'd pulled on from the bottom drawer. They were making it hard for me to breathe. And because I'm always aware of how the outer life affects the inner life, I quickly made the connection between breathing in my soul and breathing in my body.

We are not portioned-up and parceled-out people. We are whole: mind, body, and soul. Each part of us affects the other parts of us, and in order for my soul to breathe, I have to be able to actually breathe. Literally, in my diaphragm. I was wearing clothes that hurt me, and it had to stop. With a new-found clarity, I went upstairs and stood in front of my closet. We came up with a mutual understanding we could both live with. I would keep her clean and organized if she would stop harboring the enemy in the form of clothes that were too tight.

One of my favorite authors talks about this very thing. Her name is Leeana Tankersley, and in her book *Breathing Room*, she says this:

> Isn't it amazing what we will do at our own expense? I've decided that even if I have to wear something with a stretch waistband the rest of my life, I'm not going to demean myself by wearing clothes that hurt me. . . . No more bad pants. One of the ways we punish ourselves for not being more or better or thinner or stronger is by trying to squeeze ourselves—force ourselves, even—into all kinds of ill-fitting relationships. With other people, with ourselves, with our pants.[3]

I'm grateful for her words and her perspective. Those favorite jeans meant something to me, more than I had perhaps realized. They represented a version of myself I wasn't ready to let go, even if it meant I would suffer for it, literally, in my body.

In that moment, I found a new spiritual discipline.

I started to make a pile of pants and a few shirts that either physically hurt me to wear or caused me to feel bad about myself when I did. As the stack grew, so did my confidence. In those few minutes in my bedroom, I was profoundly aware of the kind presence of God with me. He doesn't stop being relevant just because I'm cleaning out my closet. And while I, of course, value taking care of my body and engaging in other practices to maintain my health, I also want to be honest about my own expectations of myself and be careful not to compare my health to the world's idea of what healthy is. I have to be careful to remember that being healthy isn't just what we can see on the outside.

If I'm honest, I struggled about making something as trivial as getting rid of pants that are too tight into a spiritual practice. It felt weird. But then I remembered how life with Christ is about being a whole person, not pieced out into important parts or unimportant parts, seen or unseen, sacred or secular. In this one day I can carry both serious concerns in my soul and a pile of old clothes to the car. Making that pile of clothes was a spiritual practice for me that day, finally taking the time to honestly confront some of the small ways I've been disrespecting myself by keeping clothes that didn't fit.

I'm calling a truce with my jeans and practicing the spiritual discipline of wearing better pants.

In an earlier chapter I mentioned that decisions are often difficult because we don't get a chance to practice them. Every decision we make feels like a final exam on the first day of class. But wearing better pants (or an equivalent personal choice) is an accessible way to begin to practice decision-making that has no consequence for anyone else but you. Again, this can be anything: a walk, an early arrival, a cup of coffee on the porch. Any small thing counts if it helps to place you in God's presence and reminds you that you are loved.

## ○ A PRAYER

*Though we may saunter into this week as people who have it all together, you see how we stumble on the inside.*

*When will we learn to stop trying to hide from you?*

*Gently reveal the complicated narrative of self-rejection that we have told ourselves all our lives. Bring the false stories to the surface, we pray.*

*Because for all the ways we have experienced healing, we know there is still so much within us that remains unseen.*

*Shine the warm light of grace into the shadows and be the courage we need to respond.*

*Hold back shame, fear, and anger with your powerful hand and extend to us your kindness.*

*We confess that we are seen and we are loved.*

*This is our truest story.*

*As we turn our face to you, may we see our true selves reflected in your gaze.*

*Open us up to a new way of practicing our life, then spin us back out into the world as people who know who we are.*

*Surprise us with a joy we cannot explain.*

*Give us the courage to show up as ourselves.*

## ○ A PRACTICE: PICK A QUIRKY SPIRITUAL DISCIPLINE

Is there anything you need to call a truce with? Nothing is off limits here. God is with you in every ordinary moment, no matter how small. Is there an unconventional spiritual practice you might need to engage in, in order to remember that? What is one thing you can do today to help you practice in your own life?

## *twenty-two*
# WALK INTO A ROOM

○  ○  ○

*The people I know who are the most con-
cerned about their individuality, who probe
constantly into motives, who are always
turned inwards toward their own reactions,
usually become less and less individual,
less and less spontaneous, more and more
afraid of the consequences of giving themselves away.*

Madeleine L'Engle, *A Circle of Quiet*

S ometimes self-reflection can get in the way. Not the kind we do in the presence of Christ—that's the important kind. But the kind practiced while looking in the mirror (or in their eyes or at their reactions). This is the kind that gets in the way of the gospel in me. If I spend too much time trying to define myself, it's easy to forget that I'm free.

In 2015 I traveled to Portland, Oregon, to speak at a writing conference. This was a job I almost said no to, not because of scheduling or money or calling or anything like that. Instead, it was because I didn't think I would be the kind of person they would like. When we get honest with ourselves, the things we base our decisions on can be embarrassing.

I had never been to Portland before, never met many of the people who I knew would be there. I thought maybe they would be young and cool hipsters and I would be not any of those things. Maybe I'd be more like the overeager page Kenneth Parcell to their cool and calm CEO Jack Donaghy. Maybe I would be the wide-eyed Jessica Day to their Nick's-cool-girlfriend Julia.[1] Maybe I would be the Hallmark Channel to their HBO. Maybe they'd write brilliantly about social justice and politics and other important issues while I wrote from my home office in my quiet cul-de-sac about creating space for your soul to breathe.

On a good day, I know my work matters. But not all days are good days. So when I was invited to speak at this conference, I hesitated. Would I have a place among these writers? Would I have anything to offer them at all? What if I was actually just fooling everyone, including myself?

This is no way to live.

For better or worse (mostly worse), this is one of my lifelong struggles. If you can't relate with that, congratulations. But if you can, I see your head nodding up and down. I know you laughed extra hard during that episode of *The Office* when Pam Beesly said she hated the idea that someone out there hates her, and that if Al-Qaeda got to know her she's sure they wouldn't hate her. This need to be liked doesn't define me, but it does tempt me and it's not as simple as just wanting to fit in. It's more like wanting to know where I fit, which is, if you can believe it, super different from wanting to fit in. I don't want to be like you, I want to be like *me*. The trouble comes when I'm not sure if being like me is good enough, acceptable, or approved of by you.

What I always come back around to, eventually, is the discovery that my job is to listen to Jesus and then to be myself no matter who else is in the room. I'm gentle by nature; I like funny TV; I think deeply about Jesus, faith, culture, grace, and people. I write to know what I think about things, but I don't write down everything I think about. I share my life on the internet, and I am deeply private. I like to be with people, and I like to be alone. I often wish I was more naturally lighthearted. Instead, I have to work at it. I like to be by myself, but I don't want to be left alone. My guess is your self-definition is about as incongruent as mine.

As it turns out, I don't have to define myself. I simply have to *be* myself. And so I said yes to speaking at this writers' conference in Portland. I settled within myself that I belonged even though I wasn't a cool hipster or a rabble-rouser or a policy maker but because I was in Christ. And the gracious people there proved those words were true.

○ ○ ○

When we are comparing, we cannot connect. It's just not possible. To some degree, we all question where we fit and how we're perceived. Don't we all work hard to protect the lingering child that still crouches within us and longs for security, worth, and love? Don't we all hope for connection but often choose protection instead? When we bring it back to discerning our next right thing today, especially if we have a decision to make, we may have a tendency to base that decision on comparison and protection rather than on a relational connection.

You may want to say no to something because you are afraid you won't measure up. Or you may be glad to say yes to something because you feel pretty confident you'll come out on top. How might your posture toward your decisions change if comparison didn't play a role at all? What if, instead of running decisions through the comparison grid, we chose to ask ourselves about *connectedness*?

I'm discovering that my understanding of spirituality, how I practice my life and how I move into the world around me, does not just inform my ministry but *is the ministry*. It begins with how I walk into a room. As I observe myself in different settings, a pattern has emerged that I am only just beginning to understand. Maybe you can relate.

When my role is clearly defined in a room, walking in is easier. If I'm hosting a birthday party for our son, I'm his mom in the room: the cake cutter, the drink getter, the chaos controller. If I'm in charge of a small group discussion, I walk into the room as the leader. If I'm attending a party, I walk in as a guest. But if my role is undefined, or if it's a social situation where I don't know people well, or if I attend a gathering where someone else in the room shares my role and the lines are unclear, I have a tendency to fly far from my center both during and after. When this scattering happens, it's often a clue that I'm living out of my false narrative fed by the temptation to be spectacular, relevant, and powerful.[2]

This is evidenced by the way I enter the room.

If I go in guarded, then I'm focused on myself and how I am perceived. When I'm attending but not in charge of the group, I often hold back and feel unsure, not wanting to seem like I'm trying to take over. As a result, I enter the room as my small, false self, wrapped up in a narrative that vacillates between uncertainty and overconfidence, from *They wouldn't want to hear from me* to *I have been doing this so much longer than the rest of these guys.* Clearly I'm a treat to be around. When I walk into a room clinging to my own false story, my body gives me hints. I get sweaty, shaky, excited, and breathless. Rather than the gathered, quiet strength available to me in Christ, I experience a physical feeling of disintegration. It's like my body knows I'm holding back and is afraid to bring my full self to the table, settling instead on a false, partial version.

When I'm hanging on to the false narrative of my own life, I walk into the room thinking, *Here I am, so what are they thinking of me?* rather than, *There you are, welcome.* I walk in lonely, looking for approval, rather than in solitude with Jesus, looking to build a connection with others. We bring what we believe about ourselves and what we believe about God into every situation, gathering, and decision.

The truth is, I don't have to let the uncertainty of my place in a room be the only voice that gets a say. How might I, in union with the Trinity, receive other people and respond as myself? How might I lean in to my identity as beloved and cooperate with the Father, Son, and Spirit by creating space for people to step out of their own false story and wake up to their unique contribution to the making-new of all creation? Even more, how might my own willingness to be vulnerable with the group be a gift, regardless of their response to me? If I walk into the room knowing who I am—beloved, abiding with the Father, the Son, and the Holy Spirit—then people are not bound to respond a certain way in order to make me feel safe. Maintaining my relational safety is not their job. If I can keep a posture of complete and absolute trust in Christ, then they are free and so am I.

o   o   o

For my part, moving forward, I don't want to live by default. I want to walk into rooms with presence and on purpose, aware of people for God's sake rather than for my sake. I want to pay attention to how all the rooms in my life may poke and prod at my desire to be relevant, spectacular, and powerful. I want to continue to imperfectly practice the spiritual discipline of letting go by refusing to try to manufacture techniques that will help me avoid failure, mishaps, and mistakes. I want to remember that true ministry is not something we do but is the overflow of an abiding life with God. I want to consider the ways I'm practicing my life so that years of sweaty, shaking discomfort don't have to go by before I realize I'm living in a false story.

I want to practice the spiritual discipline of honoring the story my body is telling me by listening to it when it's telling me the truth. I want to practice solitude more intentionally, to continue to get comfortable being alone with Jesus so I can more fully embrace my identity as beloved. I want to image

God in community through forgiveness and celebration, not in order to get acceptance but because I already have it. I want to be gentle with myself and with others, and to remember that our life with Christ is measured not with boundary lines, right practice, or perfectly made decisions but only by the love that is experienced in the Trinity and handed out to us in abundance.

Author and spiritual director Jan Johnson talks a lot about how our spiritual formation simply happens within the next ten minutes. I have been grateful to have Jan as one of my teachers in grad school, and during our residency week together she often said things like, "What would it look like to trust Jesus, to be patient, to be loving, or to be content just for the next ten minutes?" That's a next-right-thing mindset for your soul.

Maybe you'll listen before you speak.

Maybe you'll offer a smile, a nod, or a hand.

Maybe you'll simply be present with someone without an agenda.

Could it be possible that the person you're competing with most is some idealized version of yourself that you can never live up to? Would you be willing to set her free? How about just for the next ten minutes?

## ○ A PRAYER

*No matter what room we find ourselves in, help us to remember that because of Christ:*
*We are free to holler with the world changers.*
*We are free to ponder with the contemplatives.*

*We are free to campaign with the activists and be still with the liturgists.*

*We are free to be quiet and free to be loud.*

*We are free to live in the center, on the side, or in the back.*

*We are free to go.*

*We are free to stay home.*

*We are free to linger and to leave early.*

*We are free to dream big and free to dream small.*

*We are free to draw boundaries and free to change our minds.*

*There's room at the table for all of us.*

*We are free. We are free. We are free.*

*May this change how we walk into rooms.*

## ○ A PRACTICE: PAY ATTENTION TO HOW YOU WALK INTO A ROOM

When I walk into a room filled with people, I recognize in myself a tendency to ignore what God thinks of them and obsess over what they are thinking of me. I once heard author Shauna Niequist say, "With people, you can connect or you can compare, but you can't do both." Pay attention to how you walk into rooms. This mindset shift might be subtle, but it could make all the difference as you consider your underlying motivations for the choices you make. When it comes to relating with people, whether family or strangers, how you enter a room can mean the difference between connecting with them or comparing yourself to them. Try it for the next ten minutes.

# *twenty-three*
# EXPECT TO BE SURPRISED

○ ○ ○

*I don't have a five year plan. God's word is*
*a lamp unto my feet, not my football field.*

Jamie B. Golden, cohost of *The Popcast with*
*Knox and Jamie* and *The Bible Binge*

Every time I am in an airplane during takeoff, I am one part convinced the plane is going to crash and another part stunned that my childhood dream of flying has come true. The same event causes both fuzzy terror and breathtaking awe. Sometimes I even feel them at the same time.

Recently, I was on a plane that took off at sunrise, lifting us up right along with the morning. Takeoff is my least favorite part of the whole flying situation and tends to be the part where I have to focus intently so as to keep the plane in the air. I noticed the sky outside my window as we lifted up and it was lovely, to be sure, but I had the very important work of clenching my fists and breathing in deep so as to keep that airplane climbing. What would the pilot do without me? I do not ever want to find out.

As the plane continued to climb, we made a sideways turn, and the scene outside the window changed from dark early-morning sky to smoky cloud magic with cotton candy colors, pinks and golds I've never seen before or since. Glory showed up on the other side of the glass in ways I couldn't possibly explain or expect.

I'm sure you can relate to gripping the edge of your seat in an airplane or in some other area such as your kitchen or your church or your car, holding on for dear life because you don't know what will happen next, and that can be the worst part, the not knowing. But then comes a glimpse of glory you didn't expect: her perfectly timed phone call, his warm smile, a note in the mail, a kind word from a stranger, the sun rising up to kiss an airplane window. And you see it even though you weren't looking for it; you are given it even though you forgot to ask for it, this reminder that you are not invisible. A reminder that God has not forgotten and that glory is everywhere all the time, peeking out from behind warm eyes, tired hands, and pink clouds; a reminder that no matter how much we plan, list, discern, and plot, sometimes the best things that happen in life are ones we never even know are coming, much less plan for. We can be so busy willing airplanes to stay in the sky that we miss what's happening right outside the window.

It's easy to believe the myth that we are in control, especially when we have a decision to make. Turn your head from the illusion, the kind we often have when we are considering our next right thing, and see a different reality on the other side of the glass.

○  ○  ○

It's 2014 and I'm in Franklin, Tennessee, for a gathering hosted by Andrew Peterson and the Rabbit Room. It's called Hutchmoot, a funny name for a lovely weekend of live music, delicious food, and a series of discussions about art, faith, and the telling of great stories.

Someone gave me a free ticket, gifted by a friend of a friend who couldn't make it the last minute, so I'm here alone. The tickets to this particular gathering sell out in minutes each year, so to have one is a mini-miracle in itself, much less to have a free one.

I wasn't sure what to expect while here, but I knew it would be good. Yesterday I sat in the back as Luci Shaw read her poetry, took copious notes while N. D. Wilson talked about faith and art, and listened in fascination as Charlie Peacock humbly offered his perspective on fame and the culture we live in. One of my favorite moments so far came as I sat in the back of a crowded room, cookie in my hand and notebook on my lap, listening to Sally Lloyd Jones playfully read stories in her delightful English accent.

Now it's the end of the gathering, and Andrew Peterson closes with a story about a pastor who had a window in his office that was a one-way type of window, where he could see out but others couldn't see in. One day, as the pastor was working, a mother passed by with her two children. She was on the phone and stopped in front of the window, looked at her own reflection while she talked, not knowing the pastor could see her. Her face revealed her obvious displeasure with what she saw. But her two kids, who also noticed themselves in the window, moved quickly on from their own reflections and instead leaned in, cupped their hands to the glass, and noticed the pastor on the other side.

At precisely this point, Andrew ended the story. This is how he closed our weekend together, leaving us with the distracted mother on the phone frowning at her reflection and her two children cupping their faces to the window.

I deeply appreciated his decision not to wrap that story up for any of us with a moral or an explanation. The people at this gathering were not afraid to leave things open-ended, to leave space for mystery and wonder and for the Spirit to say something surprising.

Now, I didn't know it yet, but as I grabbed my bag and continued thinking about this story, I was about twenty-four hours away from a quirky serendipity that I would never know to ask for but am so pleased to have received. First, a little background.

○  ○  ○

It's hard to put into words what happens in the heart of a seventeen-year-old girl who longs for life to be poetry and beauty, when, finally, someone comes along and says it's true. If you've listened to my podcast, you likely already know who this story is about. It was my senior year of high school, and I showed up late to youth group that night. I didn't know it, but a guest musician was scheduled to sing, and the minute I saw her up there, her deep-set, mysterious eyes holding more stories than she ought to know at so young an age, I knew something was about to happen. She picked up her guitar, her small frame nearly disappearing behind it, and she began to sing.

I describe this more fully in my book *A Million Little Ways*, as it was a life-shaping moment for me. I recognized this musician didn't just sing notes; she sang *story*. For years after I first heard Sarah Masen sing that night in the youth group room of Highland Park Baptist Church in Southfield, Michigan, I found odd ways to use short lines from her lyrics as headings in my own journal and as subject lines in emails. I know it sounds weird, but at the time it was a small form of expression. Quoting her lyrics was my first timid step into discovering words of my own. Her music was the soundtrack of my freshman and sophomore years of college, and later, a line from her song "Tuesday" became the inspiration and title of one of my books, *Simply Tuesday*.

It's possible you have never heard of Sarah Masen. Maybe you've heard of her husband, writer and theologian David Dark, or her brother-in-law, Jon Foreman, the lead singer of Switchfoot. Either way, some might say she either missed or is still waiting for her big break, that she had some success in the late '90s but then she disappeared. But it all counts, all the work she did and is doing, all the time she spent creating with her music when she was younger and with her life as she grew up. The night she decided to show up to sing for those insecure high school kids was certainly not a glamorous gig. But I'm grateful she said yes to it, because I was one of those kids, walking in late, sitting in the back row, touched by the generosity of her artist's heart and her simple refusal to draw conclusions for us.

Maybe it isn't about waiting for a big break but about taking something that is alive within you and allowing it to touch the broken spots in others. Sarah's music did that for me that cold night in Michigan. It woke something up within me that hadn't yet been touched. She didn't tie up loose ends or try to explain my faith to me. She simply shared her own faith, showing up and offering her art with generosity, letting the listener decide to receive it or not. I wasn't looking for inspiration that night. But there it was, mine for the taking.

I went on to graduate from that small Michigan school, went to college for a few years in South Carolina, and then transferred to a school in North Carolina. And that's where I was, years after that first encounter, when I got word Sarah Masen was in my town to do an outdoor concert at the baseball stadium. I had no ticket, because in those days I didn't exactly have the foresight to plan ahead for things like that. Instead, the driver's seat of my little black Corolla would be the best seat I would get. I drove to the park, determined to roll down the windows and find a spot on the street close enough to the stadium to hear what I could from a distance, and I was happy to be there. As it turned out, I could hear the whole concert from my parking space, not well but good enough. Then, in the middle of her song "Come In," a couple leaving the concert early noticed me sitting small in the front seat of my car and held out an extra ticket they had. I gratefully accepted, and within minutes, the gray, muffled tones from the street became rich and distinctly colorful from inside the stadium. What had been background was now center stage.

I sat close to the front and enjoyed the music, and then afterward Sarah came into the grassy area where I stood, and we ended up chatting about how her brother and I had gone to the same small school in a suburb of Detroit, though not at the same time; about how I remembered her from a long time ago when she came to our youth group and sang folksy, poetic tunes from a stool in front, and about how I had been a fan of hers ever since.

Now, it's 2014 and Hutchmoot is over. I'm trying to decide if I should go to church before I leave town, and which church to go to if I do. Small decisions, to be sure, but after a weekend away from home and a lot of small talk, even these seem hard to untangle.

I'm not local to the area, so I consult a list they gave us and choose to attend Church of the Redeemer, since it's the church where we've been gathering this weekend and is the most familiar to me in a sea of unfamiliar options. I'm feeling nervous as I walk in, as I've been alone a lot the past few days and though I typically like that, after a while it tends to get a little, well, lonely.

I choose a seat behind a few people I recognize from our weekend together, and after the traditional Anglican service, I feel a little uncertain about lunch, not wanting to eat alone but also not wanting to spend the next five hours waiting at my gate at the airport. The waffling and back-and-forth-ness bugs me about myself. I have a rental car; I should just leave. But I'm hungry for both food and connection, so the idea of finding a restaurant and eating alone is less than appealing.

As I gather my things in slow motion to buy myself a little time to think, the people in front of me turn around and simply ask me to join them for lunch. "Come on," they say, "you can ride with us." And so I do. It wasn't in the plan and it wasn't my idea, but their simple invitation to ride along and be a part of their group was a gift to me that day. The invitation wasn't required but was certainly welcome.

As I followed them out to their car, I sensed another invitation, this one more subtle and nearly missed. *Pay attention*, it said. *Don't forget to look out the window.*

I climb into a car with three kind people I've only sort of known for a couple of days, feeling welcome and comfortable, glad to be in conversation even though we don't know each other well. After a bit of a drive, we pull up at a chicken restaurant close to Belmont.

And you might not believe me—I promise I'm not making this up—but we pull up right next to the restaurant, and there, through my backseat window, I see her at a casual outside table, sitting with her husband and family. It's Sarah Masen, eating chicken on a Sunday afternoon. In that moment I'm reminded of all the ways her music has shaped my life.

Smiling, I get out of the car. We recognize each other and chat for a bit. I meet her family and we snap a photo together. By now she knows the inspiration she's been to me. I've sent her some books; she's sent me some pottery. We're not friends, exactly, but I think we would be or at least *could* be if circumstance and place found us near one another in life.

But all that is beside the point, because you know this isn't about Sarah Masen, not really. It's about my continual insistence that I am in control of my own life. It's about the endless pressure I put on myself to make the right choice, the best choice, at the right time. I forget or maybe never truly believe how often the best things that happen are, in fact, kind gifts that have nothing to do with me. My obsession with clarity and the quick fix blinds me to all the miraculous ways Jesus works in small surprises in the midst of the long haul—through people, through connection, through his body, the church.

○ ○ ○

We make our decisions and choose our next steps, but we get scared when we can't see the future. What if we chose to finally believe that our steps are leading somewhere good? What if we see God in the yes we say even though we feel scared? What if we decided to see him in a random phone call, a kind invitation, a free ticket, a gentle nod, a hand outstretched? What if we see him from the backseat of a stranger's car as we pull up to the chicken place and call it *good*? If we continue to insist on holding on to control, we just might miss the story happening on the other side of the window. If he says he will do far more abundantly beyond all that we could ask or think, then who am I to stop before he gets there?

As we make plans, fill out lists, and do the things that need doing, may we remember still to remain open to surprise. Instead of insisting on clear plans, may we be willing to settle in and take the next right step even though it may lead someplace we didn't quite pack for. May we stop insisting that everything have an explanation. Let's be men and women who keep our ears pressed gently against the heart of God, willing to respond to faint whispers and small nudges, and even have an openness to be the wink of God for someone else.

## ○ A PRAYER

> If I go up to the heavens, you are there;
>> if I make my bed in the depths, you are there.
> If I rise on the wings of the dawn,
>> if I settle on the far side of the sea,
> even there your hand will guide me,
>> your right hand will hold me fast.
>> (Ps. 139:8–10 NIV)

*This is the Word of the Lord. Thanks be to God.*

## ○ A PRACTICE: LOOK OUT THE WINDOW

This could be metaphorical, sure. But let's start practically. The next time you ride in a car, a bus, a train, or an airplane, take some time to look out the window. Pay attention to what's happening around you and, in turn, within you. When is the last time you felt surprised by God?

# *twenty-four*
# WAIT WITH HOPE

o  o  o

*I've decided if I had my life to live over
again, I would not only climb more moun-
tains, swim more rivers, and watch more
sunsets.... I would not only go barefoot
earlier in spring and stay out later in the
fall; but I would devote not one more minute to monitoring my spiritual growth....
What would I actually do if I had it to do all
over again?... I would simply do the next
thing in love.*

Brennan Manning, *The Furious Longing of God*

On the night of March 1, 2016, American astronaut Scott Kelly arrived safely back to earth along with two other astronauts after nearly a full year on the International Space Station. I had followed his Instagram account for months by that time, amazed at his images of planet Earth from the space station. It seemed unreal, like make-believe or magic. Men and women working in *space*? Unbelievable.

Scott Kelly was part of NASA's Human Research Program, a one-year mission designed to explore the effects spending extended periods of time in space has on the human body. Even more interesting, Scott Kelly has an identical twin brother, and both men are part of a twin study conducted by NASA to find out what happens to two people with the same genes who spend time in a different environment for a year, one on earth and one in space. Needless to say, I was fascinated by this whole thing.

But the night of the return, I felt like the only person who was paying any attention. Because instead of covering Scott Kelly's return home after being the first American to spend 340 consecutive days in space, every camera in the United States was focused on one main event: results of the primary elections in several states. March 1, 2016 was also Super Tuesday.

Due to my casual obsession with this mission over the weeks before they returned, I couldn't sleep until I knew the spacecraft had landed safely. I stayed up late that night, watching nasa.gov to hear what I could about the safe arrival of Soyuz TMA-18M. It was incredibly anticlimactic, just as it should be.

This was serious scientific business. The image on the screen was mostly static, a view of the large flight control room and an occasional diagram showing where the spacecraft was at a given time. The reporting was sporadic, delivering only the facts, most of which I didn't understand, with long periods of silence in between. I waited and waited for something interesting to happen, but it all seemed rather regular, lacking the sensational feel of the political broadcasts happening everywhere else. In short, it was boring.

Even so, I was oddly grateful for the uneventful coverage. Here were grown-ups committed to their serious work. There was no ticker at the bottom, no glamorous reporters from NASA delivering interesting tidbits of information about asteroids or space travel or the moon. Just science and safety, no drama or glitz. If we wanted to watch? Fine. But this was happening whether we watched or whether we didn't. They had astronauts to bring home.

Once I heard Scott Kelly had landed safely, and as my mind hovered on the edge of sleep, I reflected for a moment on some of the election results coverage I had seen several hours earlier. I was carrying around cynicism and fear about the future of our country but I noticed within me a spark of hope and gratitude. Because our times are in the hands of God. While it takes teams of brilliant men and women to send astronauts to space and bring them back again, we have a Father who *made space*. He is our good and present God, intimately acquainted with us, our ways, our brilliance, our sin, our longings, our terror, our ideas, and all of our decisions. It's easy to forget to listen for the quietest whisper of comfort and presence from our Father who is with us in the midst of every question, every outcry, and every hope.

That night, in the fog between life and dream, I felt a string-thin thought float into my mind, drawing the loosest connection between the way that spacecraft floated onto the surface of the earth and how God snuck down one dark night as a baby, arriving while everyone was looking the other way.

○   ○   ○

There's a good chance you picked up this book because you are in a time of transition. A lot of our decision fatigue tends to show up during the pivots of life. Maybe you're a student and you struggle with the tension between the adult you are becoming and the kid they all remember. Maybe you're adjusting to a new apartment, a new city, or a new job, and you don't have a predictable routine quite yet. Maybe your kids are home from school, and your house feels unbearably loud and full, and you love them but you also need some space. Maybe you're grieving a loss, celebrating a win, or discovering something you thought was true isn't true anymore, or maybe it never was.

The kingdom of God is here, in the midst of this life stage, in the midst of this season, in the midst of this moment *right now*. There may be parts of your life where you feel like you're burying seeds again. You're holding an idea, a relationship, a loss, or a dream in the form of a seed, and you're daring to believe it will grow. So you dig into the cool dirt and drop that seed into the darkness, you cover it up, and you wait. All that would seem counterintuitive if you knew nothing of gardening, maturity, and life. Intuition says you have to hold on to these things—leave them out in the light to be displayed, produced, fixed, worked on, and planned for. This decision needs to be made, after all. But in order for the idea, the relationship, the loss, or the dream to burst forth with the light of life, first it has to be buried in the darkness of time.

You pour the clear water of hope on the mound of dirt that covers that hidden seed, which you're hoping will begin to breathe, to break, to push down roots so that it might come up green. You peer at the ground, and every day that passes without a sprout, doubt begins to grow inside your heart instead. Maybe you've done this whole thing wrong. Maybe you didn't bury it deep enough, water it enough, give it enough room to grow. Maybe you missed the seasonal window—you're too late or too early or too much or not enough. Maybe you've planted the wrong seed. Maybe you shouldn't have planted a seed at all.

In the waiting, it's easy to question and normal to doubt. But there is another reality at work, one we can't always see without help. It starts with how God moves in the world. If God had made the world straight up and down, we would have no seasons or change, just the sun shining straight at the equator all year 'round. Instead, he chose to tilt it on its axis, making a way for strawberries, red leaves, quiet snow, raging hurricanes, spring showers, and sunflowers standing high in salute. The tilt made way for long light as well as long darkness. The tilt made way for change. The earth moves, giving to some and taking from others, but then spinning around and giving something back again. When transition comes, can we take small cues from the built-in rhythm of the world?

In the morning we open the curtains to bring in the light. After days of cloud and rain, we walk outside when the sun comes out again. It's hard to capture and impossible to hold, but sitting in it, basking in it is one way we try. By the warm light of a fire, we see hope reflected in the eyes of those we love. By the glow of a burned-down candle, the dinner plates look like an art project. At midday, the patch of yellow moving slow on the living room floor is our silent company while we fold the towels.

As the sun slides gracefully through a seasonal sky, reflecting off water and windows, we consider the gift of light and all the ways God shows up in the daytime, carrying a secret message of joy. Looking out through the dim light of the world, may we continue to turn to the bright light of his presence within us. Like children emerging from the chill of an early summer swim, searching for bright patches of grass and concrete upon which to warm themselves, may we too search for the bright patches of our lives.

Am I allowing light to do what light does best—to warm, fill, and lift?

While we learn to embrace the light, may we not forget the gift of the darkness. We hold the baby, just twelve hours old, and her eyes are shut tight to defend against the world. For her, light is the stranger and *darkness* is her comforting friend. She has only known darkness within the body of her mother, and we will not take it away from her too quickly. For now, the darkness speaks of safety because that's what it is to her. We dare not push her into the light before she's ready. Her eyes will adjust in her own time and in her own way.

Am I allowing the darkness to do what the darkness does best—cover, protect, and grow?

God declares his glory in the light, but first he forms new life in the dark, bringing it to the surface in his own time and in his own way. God is with us in the light of day and in the darkest night. "Even the darkness is not dark to You, and the night is as bright as the day. Darkness and light are alike to You" (Ps. 139:12).

We want to make good decisions, but the decision is rarely the point. We want to live a good life with our good and beautiful God.[1] Doesn't it all come down to trust? We fear we'll pick wrong, turn wrong, move too soon or not soon enough. We fear we'll be out of God's will, miss his blessing, and miss our way. We fear our motives, our perception, and our place in the world.

Our decisions hang unmade around us, tiny dares waiting to call forth perfect action. They whisper possibility in the ear of the chronically hesitant among us, and we sit waiting for an answer that never comes.

Am I called to this or am I only addicted to the validation?

Do I want to marry this person or do I just want to be loved by someone?

Should I go to this school or do I just like the prestige it offers?

Who will tell us what is best?

How can we be sure?

We get into trouble when we pit two things against each other that could also coexist. You could be called to a particular job *and* be addicted to the validation. You could want to marry a certain man or woman *and* want love in unhealthy ways. You could thrive at a particular school *and* carry pride in the prestige it offers. It doesn't mean you chose wrong if (when) you discover your motives are wonky. What it does mean is there is still much to learn, you are desperately in need of Jesus, and here is where you can walk together with him toward health and wholeness.

○  ○  ○

Our next right thing will often be to wait. Give time to allow the clutter to clear. Create space for your soul to breathe. Make room for your desire to show up at the table. Begin to name the unnamed things.

Wait. Listen. Repeat.

It's not a black-and-white world, which means decisions are rarely right or wrong. It doesn't always matter which road you choose. What matters is God is with you. Sometimes I wonder if the reason he seems to move so slowly within and around us is because he knows we need time to let our blacks and whites move toward a more layered gradient of gray. When we live our lives quick, hurried, and hustled, we are prone to linear categorization. But that's the way of robots, not humans. Our hard decisions become our speed bumps, and thank God for that. Decisions are his way of saying *I love you*. It started with the Garden when he gave Adam and Eve every tree except one because he wanted them to be free. Our choices shape our lives, and they shape us. But we remain in God's hand no matter what.

Let's begin to trust ourselves as we walk with our friend Jesus.

Let's embrace the courage to choose what's best and the faith to come back when we choose what isn't.

Let's refuse to carry shame for our lack of clarity but allow our questions to linger if they need to as we wait for seeds to grow.

Let's remember that though we may have to wait and see, we never have to wait to *be*.

243

Let's bring our unknowing into the kind presence of God.

Let's continue to create space for our soul, to name the unnamed things within us, and to do our next right thing in love.

○ **A PRAYER**

*You told Abraham to leave his country, his people, and his father's household, but you didn't tell him exactly where he was going.*

*You told Moses to lead the people out of Egypt, but you didn't give him a five-week plan.*

*You told Mary she would have a Son and call him Jesus, but she wasn't offered assurance of his safety or guarantees that her life would go smoothly.*

*You are not a God who offers clear steps.*

*But you invited Abraham outside and told him to look up at the stars,* so shall your offspring be.

*You gave Moses a vision of a promised land flowing with milk and honey.*

*You whispered salvation for the whole world in Mary's ear.*

*You never promise clarity. But you always give a hopeful vision. And you always promise presence.*

I will go with you wherever you go.

Do not be afraid.

# ACKNOWLEDGMENTS

○ ○ ○

For two years this project quietly rose within me, and for months I tried to write it but I could not. The best I could do was a line here, an idea there, but nothing coherent or linear. Finally I realized the key to unlocking the mystery that was keeping me stuck. As it turned out, this material didn't want to be written, *it wanted to be spoken.*

In August 2017, I released the first episode of *The Next Right Thing* podcast and now, twenty months later, you hold in your hands what that podcast inspired. Sometimes you have to let the art tell you what it wants to be and not the other way around. What started as a podcast has now inspired a book, and I have the following people to thank for this surprising iteration of *The Next Right Thing*:

Andrea Doering and the entire team at Revell, for reaching out and making the whole thing happen in ten months' time, which feels like unicorn magic in publishing years.

Lisa Jackson, for your brilliant mix of vision casting and soul care. I can't wait to see what's next.

Anne Bogel, Ally Fallon, Claire Diaz-Ortiz, Claire Pelletreau, and Melissa Joulwan, for your vulnerability and whip-smart business ideas. The Leawood Boss Ladies: Myquillyn Smith, Caroline TeSelle, Kendra Adachi, and Tsh Oxenreider, thank you for getting it and for seeing me. And the rest of the Literary London travelers: Jamie B. Golden, Bri McKoy, and Stephanie Langford, for affirming my next right thing.

The hope*writers, for helping me pick the cover, and especially Dad and Brian Dixon, for always cheering me on.

Community 4 of The Apprentice Experience, life in the kingdom is better because I know you.

Hope Chapel, for being my people. Michael VanPatter, for asking me to read that Wendell Berry poem at The Longest Night service that one year. Without it, I'm not sure I would have ever discovered how much I enjoyed reading aloud.

Marion Gamble, for our sunroom conversations and always encouraging me to stick to the next right thing. And Beth Silvers, for helping me see the medium picture.

The listeners of *The Next Right Thing* podcast, because without you there would be no book.

Traci Hardy, for making me better. Hannah Kody, for your faithful prayers. Kendra Adachi, for your wisdom, presence, cake, well-timed GIFs, and basically everything.

Myquillyn Smith, my sister and No Mentor, for making me say yes to this book. My parents Mom, Dad, and Sherry, for love and support.

Ava, Stella, and Luke, for being the actual coolest people I know.

John, every arrow points back to you.

To God the Father, God the Son, and God the Holy Spirit, for being our narrative of hope.

# NOTES

○ ○ ○

### Chapter 1 Do the Next Right Thing

1. Alcoholics Anonymous, *Alcoholics Anonymous: The Story of How Many Thousands of Men and Women Have Recovered from Alcoholism*, 4th ed. (New York: Alcoholics Anonymous World Services, Inc., 2001), 70.

2. Susan S. Lang, "'Mindless Autopilot' Drives People to Dramatically Underestimate How Many Daily Food Decisions They Make, Cornell Study Finds," *Cornell Chronicle*, December 22, 2006, http://news.cornell .edu/stories/2006/12/mindless-autopilot-drives-people-underestimate-food -decisions.

### Chapter 2 Become a Soul Minimalist

1. *Minimalism: A Documentary About the Important Things*, directed by Matt D'Avella (Catalyst, 2015), documentary; https://minimalismfilm.com/.

2. Tsh Oxenreider and Joshua Becker, "The More of Less," *The Art of Simple* (audio blog), June 11, 2016, https://theartofsimple.net/podcast /30/.

3. A. J. Swoboda, "Incarnational Tradition," lecture, June 28, 2018, History and Traditions of Christian Spiritual Formation (online class), Friends University.

4. Andy Crouch, *The Tech-Wise Family: Everyday Steps for Putting Technology in Its Proper Place* (Grand Rapids: Baker Books, 2017).

### Chapter 3 Name the Narrative

1. Madeleine L'Engle, *Walking on Water: Reflections on Faith and Art* (New York: Convergent Books, 2016), 102.

2. CNN, "@ThisHour with Berman and Michaela: Obama Heads to NATO Summit; Ebola Survivor Nancy Writebol Speaks Out; Cease-fire in Ukraine or No?" *CNN Transcripts*, September 3, 2014, http://edition.cnn.com /TRANSCRIPTS/1409/03/ath.01.html.

### Chapter 4 Picture God

1. According to Gary Black in his book *Discovering Protoevangelical Faith*, this statement is considered one of Dallas Willard's most memorable pieces of wisdom.

### Chapter 5 Look for Arrows

1. Ann Patchett, *What Now?* (New York: Harper, 2008), 77.

2. Dallas Willard, *The Divine Conspiracy: Rediscovering Our Hidden Life in God* (New York: HarperOne, 2018).

3. Dallas Willard, *Hearing God: Developing a Conversational Relationship with God* (Brookfield, WI: Dolan Productions, LLC, 2011), 261.

4. Willard, *Hearing God*, 261.

### Chapter 8 Know What You Want More

1. Ruth Haley Barton, *Sacred Rhythms* (Downers Grove, IL: InterVarsity Press, 2006), 23.

### Chapter 10 Quit Something

1. Greg McKewon, *Essentialism* (New York: Crown, 2014), 5.

2. David Benner, *The Gift of Being Yourself* (Downers Grove, IL: Inter-Varsity Press, 2008), 88.

3. Adam S. McHugh, *The Listening Life: Embracing Attentiveness in a World of Distraction* (Downers Grove, IL: IVP Books, 2015), 185.

### Chapter 11 Stay in Today

1. Ted Loder, "Gather Me to Be with You," *Guerrillas of Grace: Prayers for the Battle, 20th Anniversary Edition* (Minneapolis: Augsburg Books, 2005), 76.

2. Eugene H. Peterson, *The Jesus Way: A Conversation on the Ways That Jesus Is the Way* (Grand Rapids: Eerdmans, 2011), 97.

## Chapter 13 Don't Rush Clarity

1. Marie Forleo, "You Can't Rush Clarity or Force Growth. Cultivate Patience. #Trusttheprocess," Twitter post, March 6, 2018, twitter.com/marie forleo/status/971074693137682437.

2. Marie Forleo, "The Secret to Finding Your Passion (Hint: It's Not What You Think)," Oprah.com, November 14, 2012, www.oprah.com/supersoul sunday/the-secret-to-finding-your-passion-hint-its-not-what-you-think.

## Chapter 15 Gather Co-Listeners

1. Parker J. Palmer, "The Clearness Committee," *Center for Courage & Renewal*, accessed October 31, 2018, www.couragerenewal.org/clearness committee/.

## Chapter 17 Find a No Mentor

1. My sister, Myquillyn Smith, is the ultimate No Mentor. You can find her at thenester.com.

## Chapter 19 Come Home to Yourself

1. Macrina Weidekehr, *Seasons of Your Heart* (New York: HarperOne, 1991), 71.

## Chapter 21 Wear Better Pants

1. If you find yourself struggling with some version of the good girl who lives in your head, who tells you that if you could just try harder you would be a better version of yourself, you might enjoy my book *Grace for the Good Girl*. It is all about learning to let go of your try-hard life. There is also a version for teen girls (mainly high school students) called *Graceful*. You can find these and more at emilypfreeman.com/the-books.

2. Dallas Willard, *Living in Christ's Presence* (Downers Grove, IL: InterVarsity Press, 2017), 151.

3. Leeana Tankersley, *Breathing Room* (Grand Rapids: Revell, 2014), 141–42.

## Chapter 22 Walk into a Room

1. Kenneth Parcell and Jack Donaghy are characters on the show *30 Rock* that ran on NBC from 2006–2013. Kenneth is the always-smiling, overeager NBC page, and Jack is the cool and confident CEO. Jessica Day and Nick's girlfriend, Julia, are characters on the show *New Girl* that ran on FOX from 2011–18. Julia's glass is always half empty; Jess's is always half full.

2. Henri Nouwen talks about these three temptations of Jesus in his book *In the Name of Jesus: Reflections on Christian Leadership* (Hong Kong: Logos Book House, 1992).

### Chapter 24  Wait with Hope

1. Author James Bryan Smith wrote an entire series about life with God, the good and beautiful. Start with the first one, *The Good and Beautiful God* (Downers Grove, IL: InterVarsity Press, 2009).

**Emily P. Freeman** is the *Wall Street Journal* bestselling author of *Simply Tuesday* and *A Million Little Ways*. She is also the host of *The Next Right Thing* podcast, which is designed to help anyone struggling with decision fatigue to simply do the next right thing in love. With an MA in Christian spiritual formation and leadership, Emily always seeks to create space for the soul to breathe, offering fresh perspective on the sacredness of our inner life with God. Emily and her husband, John, live in North Carolina with their twin daughters, Ava and Stella, and their son, Luke. Connect with her online at emilypfreeman.com and on Instagram @emilypfreeman.

# The Next Right Thing Podcast

Want a weekly reminder to create space for your soul
to breathe so you can discern your next right thing?
Listen in each week for a short reflection, a simple
action, and a thoughtful benediction.

Visit **thenextrightthingpodcast.com**
to listen or subscribe in your favorite
podcast listening app.

connect with

# EMILY

○ ○ ○

emilypfreeman.com

 EmilyFreemanAuthor

 emilypfreeman

 emilypfreeman

# DISCOVER THE *Meaning* IN EACH MOMENT

with These Books by Emily P. Freeman